The WONDERFUL WORLD of MAPS

by
James F. Madden

CONTENTS

HOW TO READ MAPS

MAPS OF THE WORLD

Library of Congress Cataloging in Publication Data
Madden, James F
   The wonderful world of maps.
   Includes index.
   1. Maps—Juvenile literature.   I. Hammond Incorporated
   II. Title.
GA130.M35   912   77-24310
ISBN 0-8437-3411-6

HAMMOND
INCORPORATED

Printed in the United States of America
   MAPLEWOOD, NEW JERSEY   07040

FACTS ABOUT OUR EARTH

THE EARTH IS A PLANET

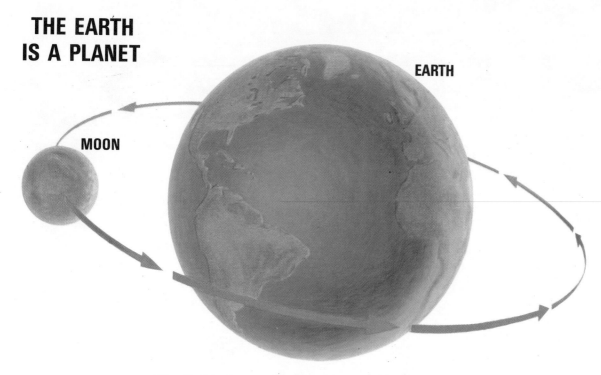

The EARTH is a PLANET. We all live on the planet earth. A planet is a large solid body that moves through space around the SUN. From the sun the earth receives its light and heat. The earth is one of the nine planets of our solar system.

Our nearest neighbor in space is the MOON. The moon joins us as we move around the sun. No one lives on the moon. But astronauts have visited the moon.

DIAMETERS OF THE PLANETS AND SUN

The sun is much larger than the earth or other planets of our solar system. This is how the planets would look if they were placed next to the sun's edge.

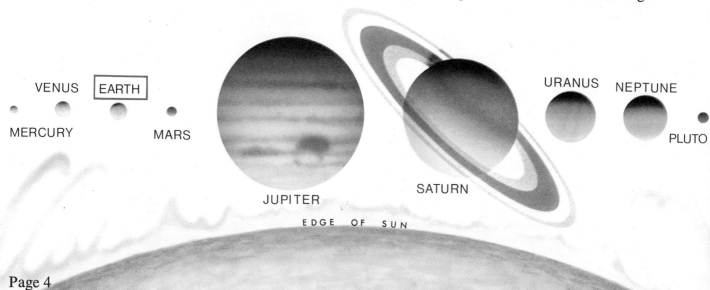

ROTATION

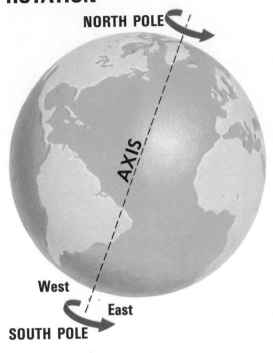

NORTH POLE

AXIS

West

East

SOUTH POLE

GYROSCOPE
a spinning top

Our earth turns around, or ROTATES, in a west to east direction. It always leans a little, or is tilted, to one side. It rotates on its axis like a spinning gyroscope or top. The axis is an imaginary line that runs through the center of the earth. The ends of the axis are the North Pole and the South Pole. The spinning, or ROTATION, of the earth causes night and day.

NIGHT AND DAY

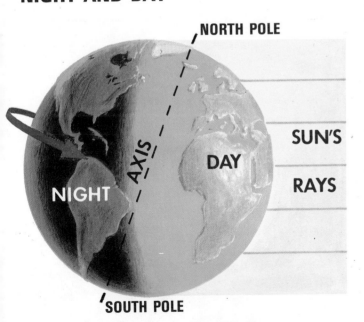

NORTH POLE

NIGHT

AXIS

DAY

SUN'S

RAYS

SOUTH POLE

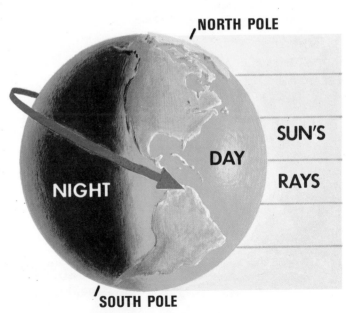

NORTH POLE

NIGHT

DAY

SUN'S

RAYS

SOUTH POLE

The earth turns or rotates on its axis once a day, or once every 24 hours. When our part of the earth is turned away from the sun, it is NIGHT. When our part of the earth faces the sun, it is DAY. We are carried by the spinning earth from nighttime to daytime and, about 12 hours later, to nighttime again.

MORE FACTS ABOUT OUR EARTH

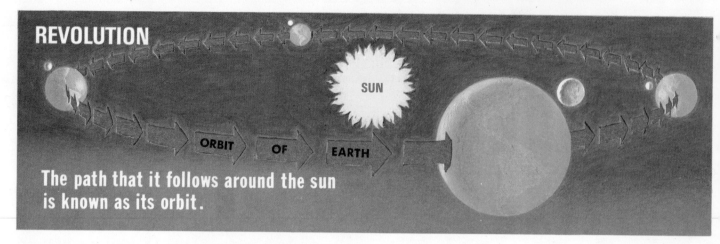

REVOLUTION

SUN

ORBIT OF EARTH

The path that it follows around the sun is known as its orbit.

The earth is always moving. Besides spinning like a top, it also takes a journey around the sun. It travels, or REVOLVES, around the sun. The path that the earth follows is known as its orbit. It takes the earth one year, or actually 365¼ days, to make one complete REVOLUTION around the sun.

Think of the earth as a ball being whirled around on the end of a string. The string keeps the ball from flying away. In a similar way, the sun keeps the earth from flying away. The sun is like a strong magnet. The strong attraction of the sun keeps the earth in its orbit and from flying off into outer space.

SPHERE

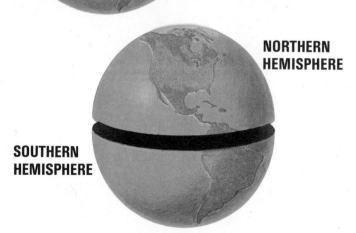

HEMISPHERES

The earth is a SPHERE. A sphere is a figure that is round like a ball or globe. The earth can be divided into HEMISPHERES. "Hemi" comes from a Greek word that means "half of." A hemisphere is half of a sphere or half of the earth. In the United States, we live in the Northern Hemisphere. We also live in the Western Hemisphere.

NORTHERN HEMISPHERE

SOUTHERN HEMISPHERE

EASTERN HEMISPHERE

WESTERN HEMISPHERE

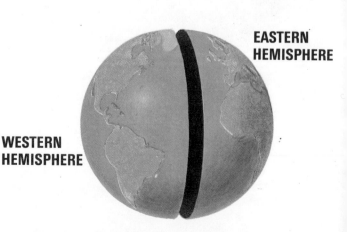

SEASONS

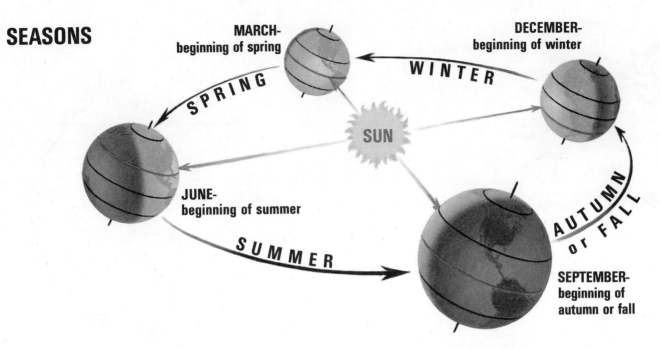

MARCH-
beginning of spring

DECEMBER-
beginning of winter

WINTER

SPRING

SUN

JUNE-
beginning of summer

SUMMER

AUTUMN or FALL

SEPTEMBER-
beginning of
autumn or fall

As the earth spins on its tilted axis, it also travels around the sun. This is what gives us our SEASONS. When the northern half of the earth, or Northern Hemisphere, leans toward the sun, we have summer. Daylight lasts longer then. When the Northern Hemisphere leans away from the sun, we have winter. There are fewer hours of daylight in winter.

When the southern half of the earth, or the Southern Hemisphere, leans toward the sun, it has summer and we have winter. In the Southern Hemisphere the seasons are always the opposite of ours.

One part of the earth is always hot. This is the region near the equator. Here the sun shines bright and hot all year. It receives the direct rays of the sun. We call this region the Tropical Region.

The two areas, or zones, that lie on each side of the Tropical Region receive the sun's rays at an angle. This causes a cooler and more moderate climate. Here the seasons change. We live in the northern zone of the moderate climate.

The polar regions are cold all year round. They are the coldest parts of the earth.

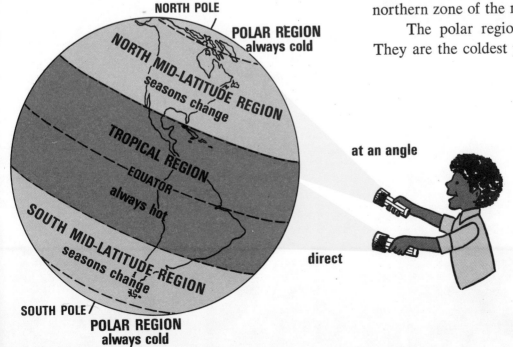

NORTH POLE

POLAR REGION
always cold

NORTH MID-LATITUDE REGION
seasons change

TROPICAL REGION

EQUATOR
always hot

SOUTH MID-LATITUDE REGION
seasons change

SOUTH POLE

POLAR REGION
always cold

at an angle

direct

WHAT A MAP IS

PHOTOGRAPH OF THE EARTH FROM SPACE

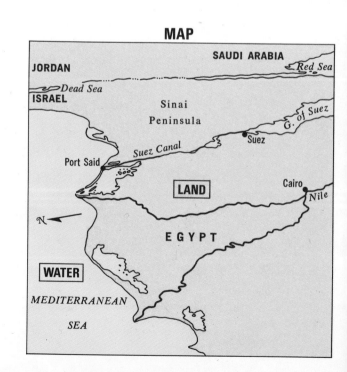

GLOBE

A doll is a model of a person. A toy airplane is a model of a real airplane. In the same way, a globe is a model of the earth. A globe shows the roundness of the earth. It shows all the lands and seas in their true shapes and positions. A globe is actually a map of the world.

A MAP is like a picture of the earth taken from high in the air or from space. The photograph below shows a part of the earth as it looks from a satellite circling the earth. Next to it is a map of the same area. The map is another kind of picture or diagram of this area.

A map can show the land and water areas of the earth. It can also show many things that are located upon the land areas.

PHOTOGRAPH

MAP

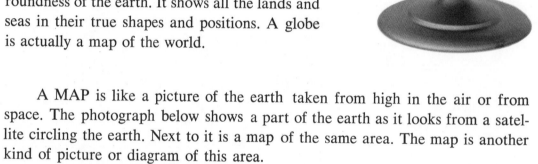

WHAT A MAP CAN SHOW

Maps can show the natural features of the earth. Natural features are things that were made by nature. They make up the land and water areas of the earth. Natural features include such things as mountains, oceans, islands, rivers, and lakes. What other natural features can you think of that could be shown on maps?

NATURAL FEATURES

Maps can also show man-made features. They are things that are made or built on the earth's surface by people. Cities, towns, bridges, tunnels, airports, and dams are some examples of man-made features. Name some other man-made features that could be shown on a map.

MAN-MADE FEATURES

Some maps show routes or highways. This kind of information is of great help to people who travel by car. The routes or highways that connect our towns and cities are marked by numbers. By following a certain marked highway, the traveler can be guided from one town to another. Highways are man-made features.

ROUTES

SYMBOLS

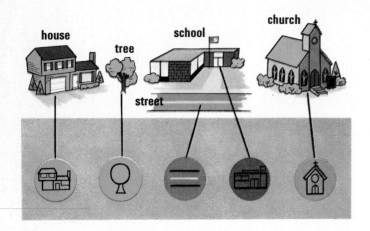

A SYMBOL "stands for something." Map-makers use small drawings, or symbols, to stand for different things when they make their maps. A symbol often looks like or suggests the feature it stands for. Look at the detailed pictures of the house, school, and church. Now look at the simple drawings. You can easily recognize what each symbol stands for.

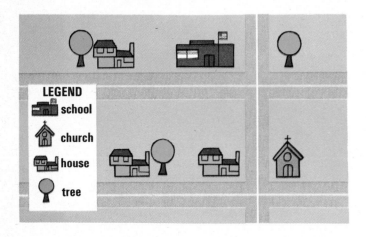

A map usually has a legend or key. A key is the information that solves a problem. On a map this explanation is found in the legend or key. Each symbol is explained so you will know what it stands for on the map.

On the map below, look at the symbols in the legend. The symbols do not look exactly like the actual features they stand for, but they are still easily understood. What things can you find in the picture that are not shown on the map?

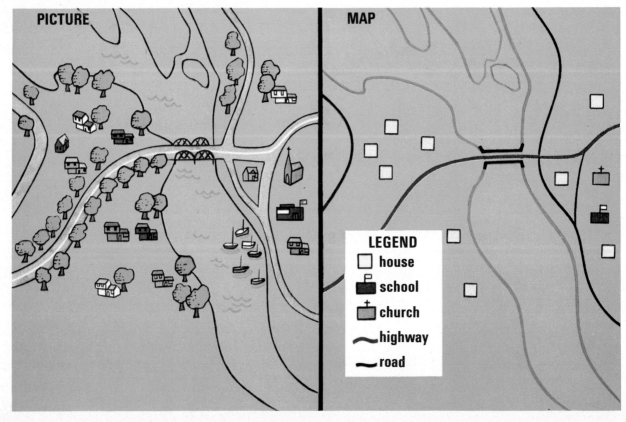

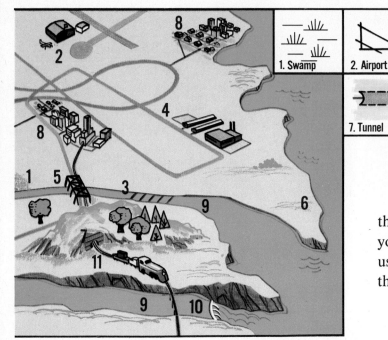

1. Swamp	2. Airport	3. Canal	4. Roads	5. Bridge	6. Coastline
7. Tunnel	8. Towns—Cities	9. Rivers	10. Dam	11. Railroad	

In some ways, map symbols are like letters of the alphabet. If you can understand the symbols, you can read a map as you would read a book. By using symbols, mapmakers can tell you much about the natural and man-made features on the earth.

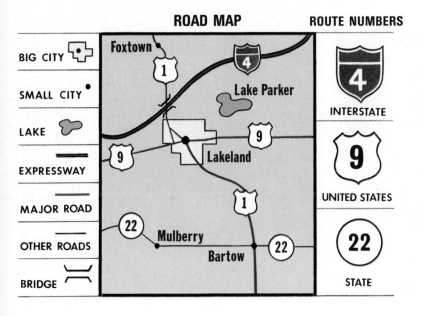

ROAD MAP   **ROUTE NUMBERS**

BIG CITY

SMALL CITY

LAKE

EXPRESSWAY

MAJOR ROAD

OTHER ROADS

BRIDGE

INTERSTATE

UNITED STATES

STATE

A road map is a special kind of map. Road maps will help guide you to where you want to go. These maps use special symbols, or route numbers, to identify the roads and highways. There is a uniform system of numbering the roads and highways throughout the United States. Why do you think this uniform system of numbering highways is necessary? Look at the small road map at the left. What United States numbered highway would you take to get from Foxtown to Bartow?

A SELECTION OF MAP SYMBOLS USED IN ATLASES

International Boundary   Lake   ▲ Mountain Peak   Roads

Other Boundary   Seasonal Lake)(Mountain Pass   Route Numbers

Capital of Country   Dry Lake

Other Capital   Canal

City or Town   Swamp

River   Desert

Seasonal River   Ruins

The symbols shown here are some of the most often used map symbols. By using symbols, a mapmaker can show a large amount of information in a small area.

DIRECTION

Rocket lift-off

UP

DOWN

Capsule landing

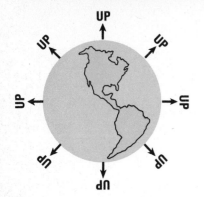

The word DIRECTION means "which way." The direction UP means up into the air, or away from the earth's surface.

The direction DOWN means down toward the water and land, or toward the earth's surface.

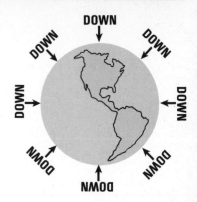

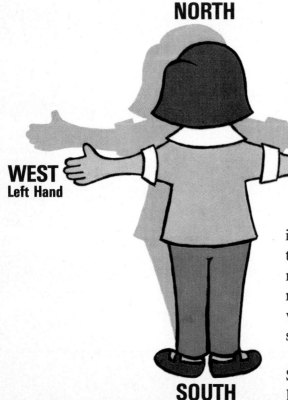

NORTH

WEST
Left Hand

EAST
Right Hand

SOUTH

Compass

There are different ways to find other directions. One way is by using your shadow. At noon, if you stand with your back to the sun, your shadow will point NORTH. Directly opposite north is SOUTH. Your back will be toward the south. If you raise your arms, your left arm will point WEST. Your right arm will point EAST. The sun appears to rise in the east at dawn and set in the west at nightfall.

Another way of finding directions is by using a compass. Scouts use a compass when they go on a hike. If a compass is held flat, the needle will point north.

A MAP TELLS DIRECTION

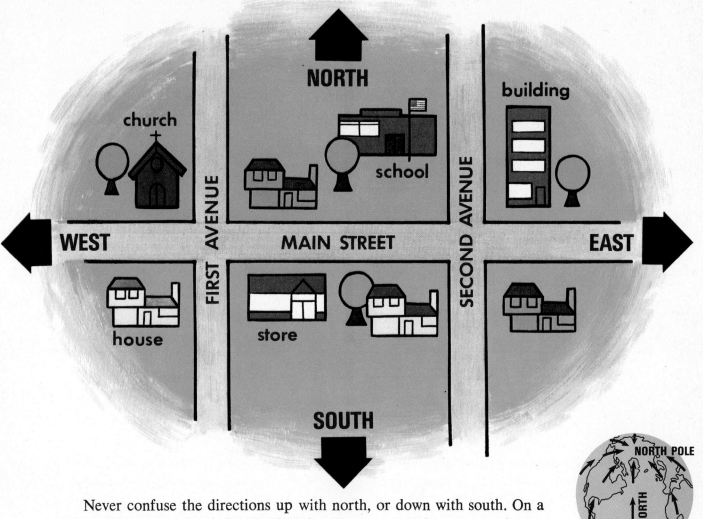

Never confuse the directions up with north, or down with south. On a map north means toward the North Pole. If you travel from any point on the earth's surface toward the North Pole, you are going north. The North Pole is the point farthest north on the earth's surface.

The South Pole is the point farthest south on the earth's surface. If you travel from any point on the earth's surface toward the South Pole, you are going south.

A map tells you in which direction one object or place is from another. Look at the picture map above. What color house is north of the store? In which direction is the building from the school? In which directions does Main Street run?

Maps usually do not have the direction north spelled out for you. Most maps have a COMPASS ROSE that tells you where north is located on the map.

DISTANCE

12" or 1 FOOT

The word DISTANCE means "how far." The distance between two places means how far away one place is from the other. Suppose you wanted to know the distance between two walls of your schoolroom. You might count how many steps one wall is from the other. This would give you some idea of the distance between the two walls. A more accurate way to measure is to use a ruler or a measuring tape. But no one can measure *long* distances by using a ruler or a measuring tape.

Sometimes people measure distances in feet. Look at the picture above. How many inches are there in one foot?

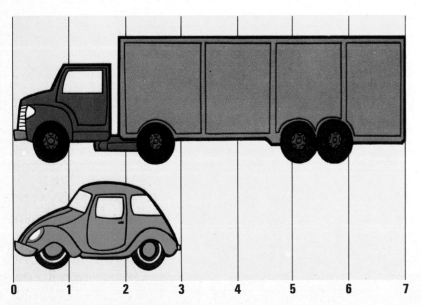

People also measure distances in meters. Look at the drawing at the left. How long is the small car? How long is the truck?

0 1 2 3 4 5 6 7

DISTANCE OR LENGTH IN METERS

A MAP TELLS DISTANCE

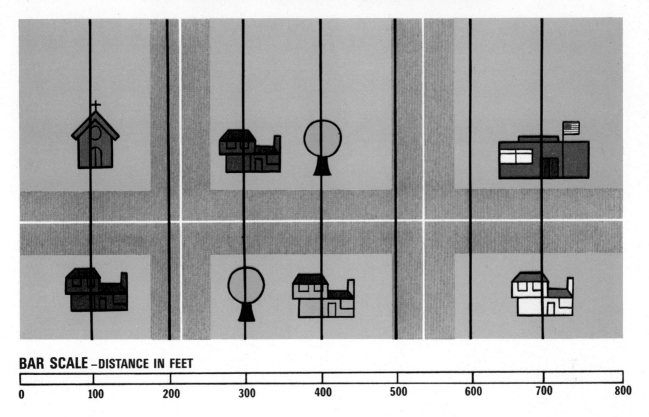

BAR SCALE – DISTANCE IN FEET

0	100	200	300	400	500	600	700	800

A map can be used to tell distance when it has a BAR SCALE. A bar scale is like a ruler or measuring tape. You can measure *long* distances with a bar scale. The map above has a bar scale marked off into eight equal parts. Each part is equal to 100 feet. Using the bar scale, you could measure the distance between the blue house and the yellow house as about 300 feet. What is the distance between the church and the school?

MEASURING DISTANCE ON A MAP BY USING A BAR SCALE

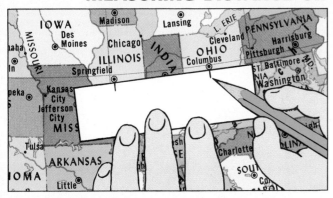

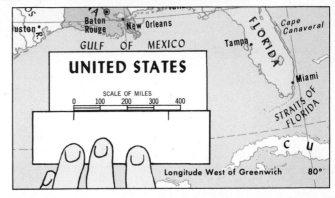

The maps above show a student using a bar scale to find the distance between Springfield, Illinois, and Columbus, Ohio. First, he locates the dots indicating the two cities on his map. Then he marks off the space between them on the edge of a cardboard strip. Next, he places the cardboard on the bar scale of the map so that the first mark is at zero. The second mark falls about halfway between 300 and 400. This bar scale is marked off into miles. The student knows that the distance in a straight line between the two cities is about 350 miles. The distance may be much longer if you travel by road. Why do you think the actual road distance may be longer?

WHAT SCALE MEANS

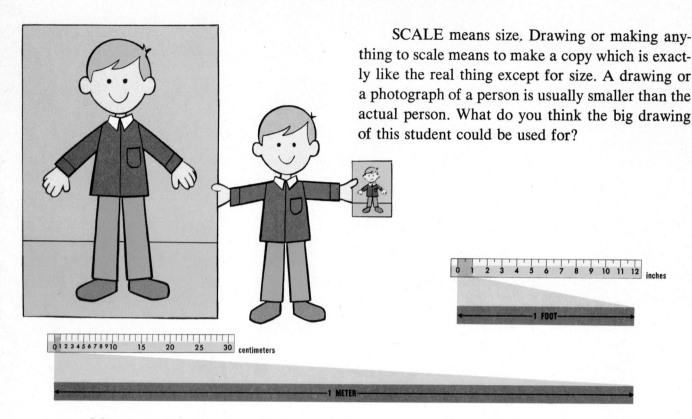

SCALE means size. Drawing or making anything to scale means to make a copy which is exactly like the real thing except for size. A drawing or a photograph of a person is usually smaller than the actual person. What do you think the big drawing of this student could be used for?

Maps are scale drawings or plans of places. A map of a country, a city, or even a room would be much too large to use if it were drawn to exactly the same size as the place really is. To make a map of convenient size, mapmakers let a small length, such as an inch, stand for a large one, such as a foot or a mile. In the same way, a centimeter could stand for a meter or a kilometer. The two maps below show exactly the same area. But they are drawn to different scales.

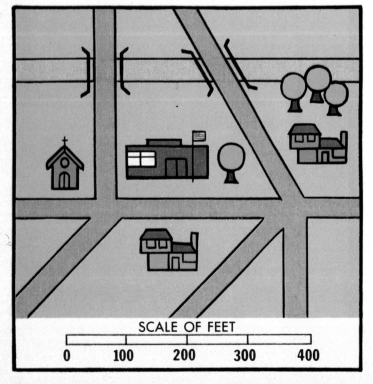

SCALE OF FEET

0   100   200   300   400

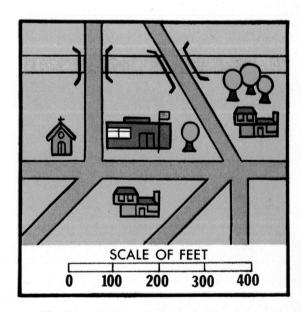

SCALE OF FEET

0   100   200   300   400

If the metric system were used, the scales of these two maps would be shown in meters instead of feet. On page 17 the scales would be in meters and kilometers.

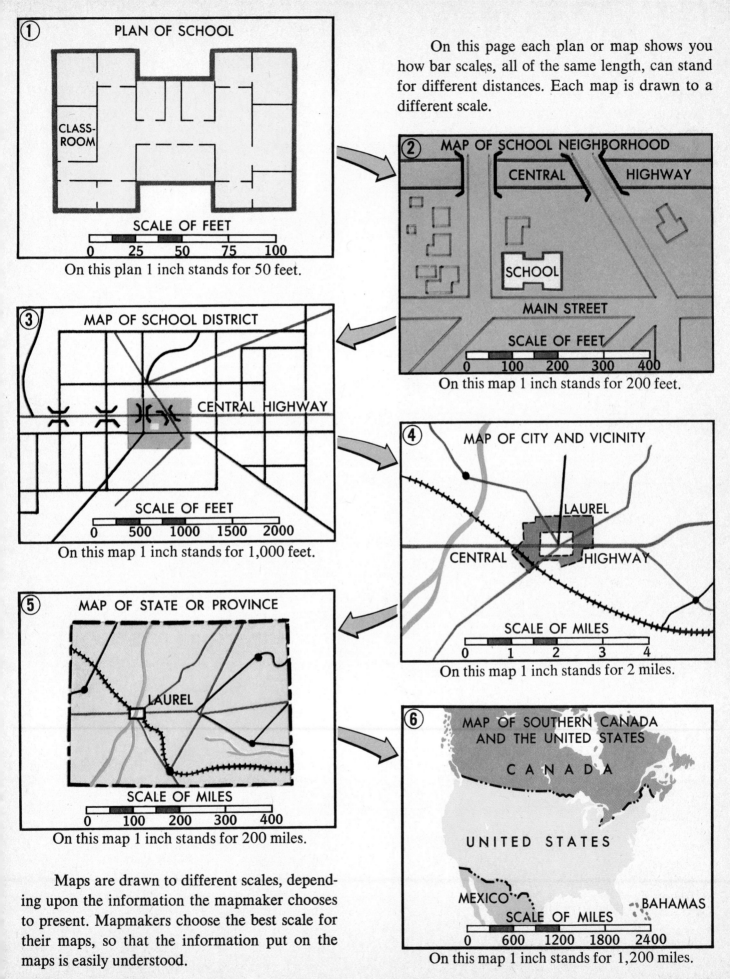

① PLAN OF SCHOOL

CLASS-ROOM

SCALE OF FEET

0   25   50   75   100

On this plan 1 inch stands for 50 feet.

On this page each plan or map shows you how bar scales, all of the same length, can stand for different distances. Each map is drawn to a different scale.

② MAP OF SCHOOL NEIGHBORHOOD

CENTRAL   HIGHWAY

SCHOOL

MAIN STREET

SCALE OF FEET

0   100   200   300   400

On this map 1 inch stands for 200 feet.

③ MAP OF SCHOOL DISTRICT

CENTRAL HIGHWAY

SCALE OF FEET

0   500   1000   1500   2000

On this map 1 inch stands for 1,000 feet.

④ MAP OF CITY AND VICINITY

LAUREL

CENTRAL   HIGHWAY

SCALE OF MILES

0   1   2   3   4

On this map 1 inch stands for 2 miles.

⑤ MAP OF STATE OR PROVINCE

LAUREL

SCALE OF MILES

0   100   200   300   400

On this map 1 inch stands for 200 miles.

Maps are drawn to different scales, depending upon the information the mapmaker chooses to present. Mapmakers choose the best scale for their maps, so that the information put on the maps is easily understood.

⑥ MAP OF SOUTHERN CANADA AND THE UNITED STATES

C A N A D A

U N I T E D   S T A T E S

MEXICO   BAHAMAS

SCALE OF MILES

0   600   1200   1800   2400

On this map 1 inch stands for 1,200 miles.

Page 17

USING COLOR AS A SYMBOL

Remember that a symbol "stands for something." The maps on pages 18 and 19 use colors as symbols. The colors stand for something. Each color has a special meaning. The legends explain what each color stands for.

WARM AND COLD LANDS IN JANUARY

What the colors stand for...

LEGEND

Very cold lands

Cold lands

Cool lands

Warm lands

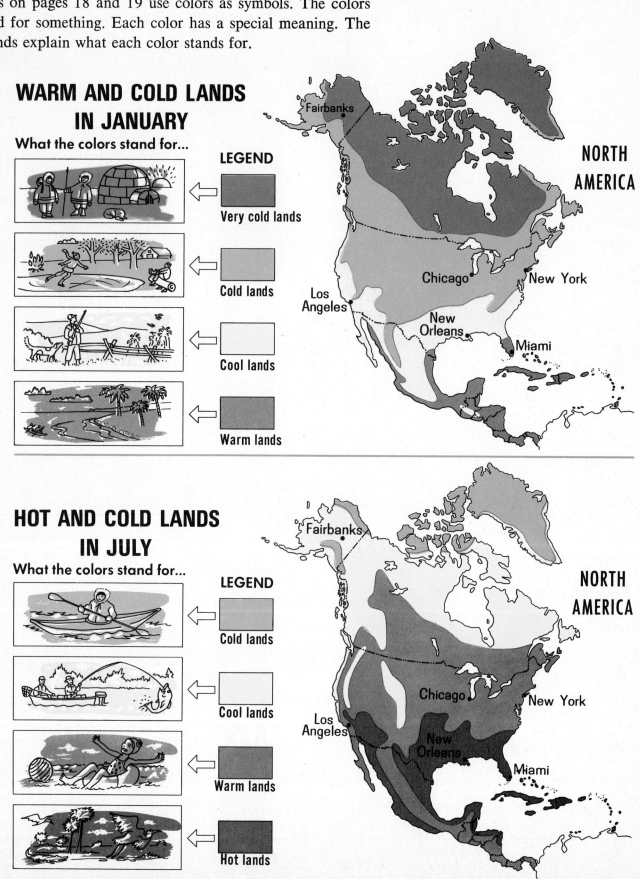

NORTH AMERICA

Fairbanks

Chicago

New York

Los Angeles

New Orleans

Miami

HOT AND COLD LANDS IN JULY

What the colors stand for...

LEGEND

Cold lands

Cool lands

Warm lands

Hot lands

NORTH AMERICA

Fairbanks

Chicago

New York

Los Angeles

New Orleans

Miami

Look at the two maps below. They are maps of the world. Again, the colors stand for something. Here, the colors stand for degrees of temperature. Do these maps give you the same kind of information as the maps on page 18? What other kinds of information can a mapmaker show on a map by using colors?

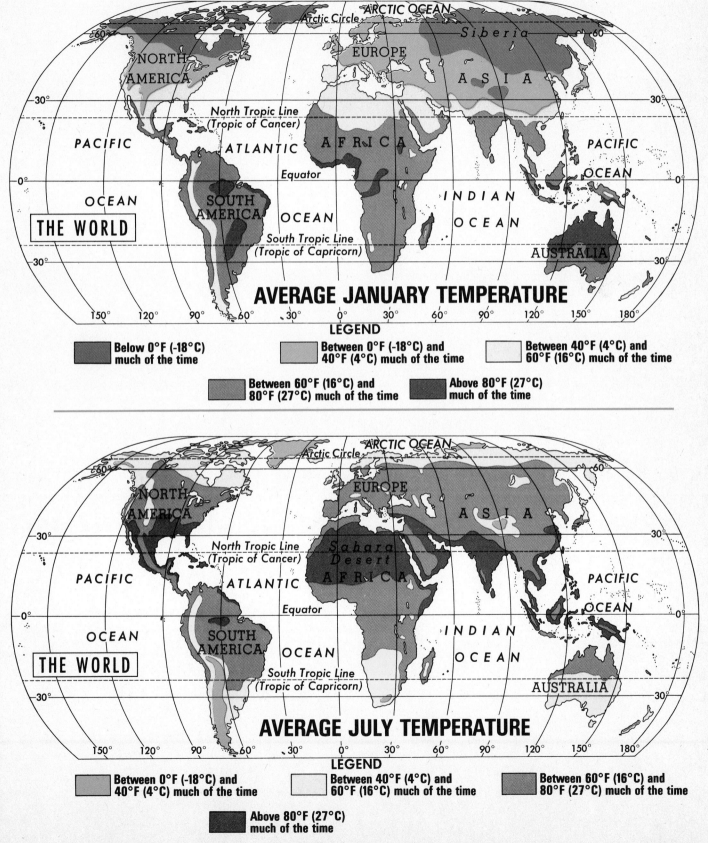

THE WORLD

AVERAGE JANUARY TEMPERATURE

LEGEND

Below 0°F (-18°C) much of the time	Between 0°F (-18°C) and 40°F (4°C) much of the time	Between 40°F (4°C) and 60°F (16°C) much of the time
Between 60°F (16°C) and 80°F (27°C) much of the time	Above 80°F (27°C) much of the time	

THE WORLD

AVERAGE JULY TEMPERATURE

LEGEND

Between 0°F (-18°C) and 40°F (4°C) much of the time	Between 40°F (4°C) and 60°F (16°C) much of the time	Between 60°F (16°C) and 80°F (27°C) much of the time
Above 80°F (27°C) much of the time		

RELIEF OR PHYSICAL MAPS

If you want to study a particular land and its people, you must learn about the geography of the land. Some maps are made just for this purpose. They show mountains, highlands, and lowlands. This type of map is called a RELIEF or PHYSICAL map. It shows the physical or natural features of the land.

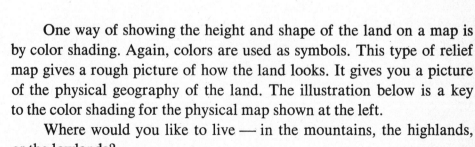

One way of showing the height and shape of the land on a map is by color shading. Again, colors are used as symbols. This type of relief map gives a rough picture of how the land looks. It gives you a picture of the physical geography of the land. The illustration below is a key to the color shading for the physical map shown at the left.

Where would you like to live — in the mountains, the highlands, or the lowlands?

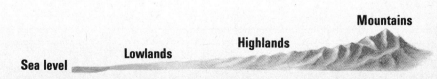

LAND AND SEA IN PICTURE AND MAP

The drawing below is a map of the picture shown above. Compare one with the other. This will help you understand how maps are drawn and in map reading. This map shows both natural features (like lakes or mountains) and man-made features.

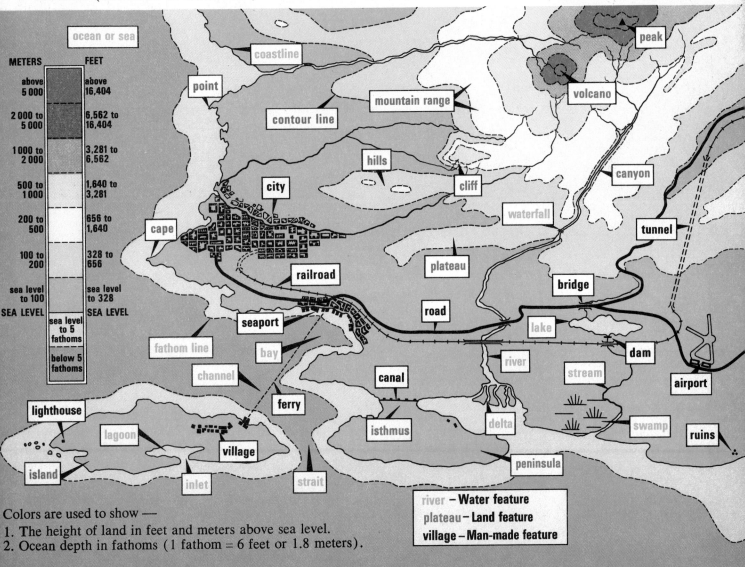

Colors are used to show —
1. The height of land in feet and meters above sea level.
2. Ocean depth in fathoms (1 fathom = 6 feet or 1.8 meters).

POLITICAL MAPS

Here is an outline of the land area of 48 of the 50 states that make up the United States of America. Many peoples have come here to live. All have helped to build one great country or nation. The United States is a nation. A POLITICAL MAP can show nations.

Boundaries are imaginary lines that mark the limits of certain areas. On a political map, lines that tell you where one nation ends and another begins are called INTERNATIONAL BOUNDARIES. The nation to the north of the United States is Canada. The nation to the south of the United States is Mexico.

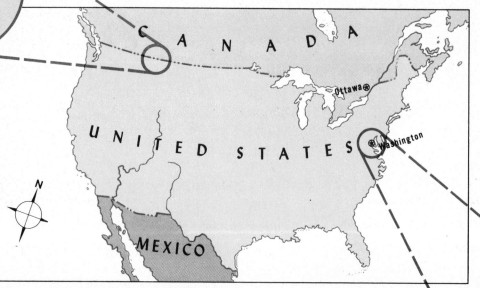

Each nation has a city where its central government is located. These cities are called NATIONAL CAPITALS. A few nations have two national capitals. Look at the map. What city is the national capital of the United States?

The building with the high dome is the United States Capitol. This is where the houses of Congress meet to determine the laws of our land.

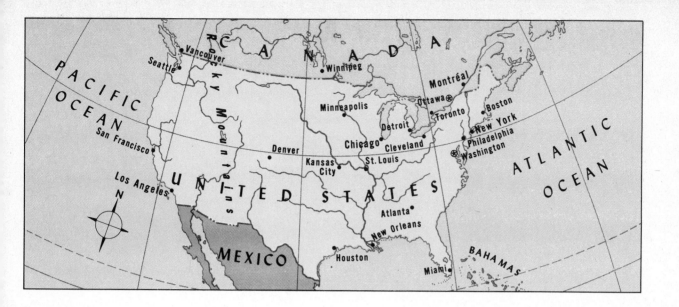

The map above is a section of the political map of North America. You can see that it shows other major cities besides national capitals. What symbol is used to show these other cities? The principal land and water features are also named. You will find the complete political map of North America on page 31.

Some political maps show state boundaries and state capitals. Do you know the capital of your state? See page 35 for the political map of the United States.

Some large political maps include additional transportation features, such as highways, airplane routes, and railroads.

When a map shows both the physical features and the political features of an area, it is called a physical-political map. See page 58 for the physical-political map of the Pacific Ocean area.

Some maps show details of streets. How would you show crosswalks like these on a map?

This city is Chicago, Illinois. Find Chicago on the map at the top of this page. What lake is it located on? Why do you think big cities build skyscrapers?

LATITUDE AND LONGITUDE

LATITUDE

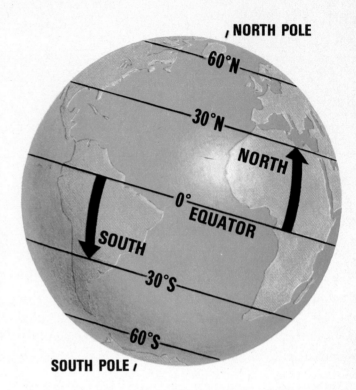

Mapmakers and geographers use lines of latitude and lines of longitude to locate places on the earth's surface. Lines of LATITUDE, or parallels, are imaginary lines running east-west around the earth. These lines are sometimes called parallels of latitude. They are like circles drawn around a ball. Latitude is measured in degrees (°) north or south of the equator. The equator is 0° Latitude.

LONGITUDE

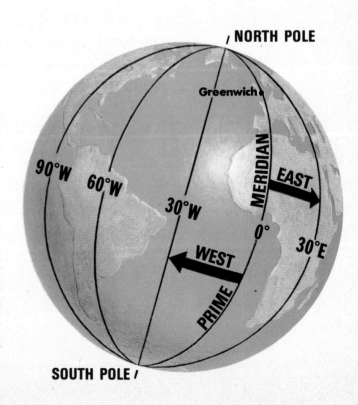

Lines of LONGITUDE, or meridians, are imaginary lines running north-south from the poles. These lines are sometimes called meridians of longitude. They are like half circles drawn around a ball. Longitude is measured in degrees (°) east or west of the prime meridian. The prime meridian, or first meridian, is 0° Longitude. Greenwich, England, is located on the prime meridian.

EARTH'S GRID

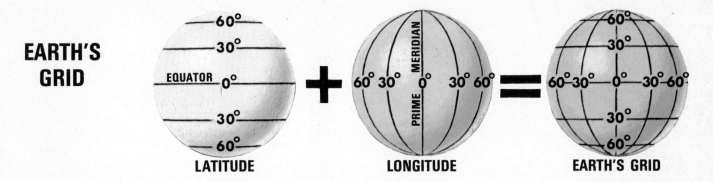

LATITUDE   +   LONGITUDE   =   EARTH'S GRID

Let's review once again. Latitude tells you how far north or south of the equator a place is located. Longitude tells you how far east or west of the prime meridian a place is located.

When lines of latitude and lines of longitude are placed together, they form the EARTH'S GRID. This grid, or network of lines, makes it possible to find the location of any place on the earth's surface.

Look at lines of latitude and lines of longitude on a globe. Notice that lines of latitude never meet, but lines of longitude meet at the North and South poles.

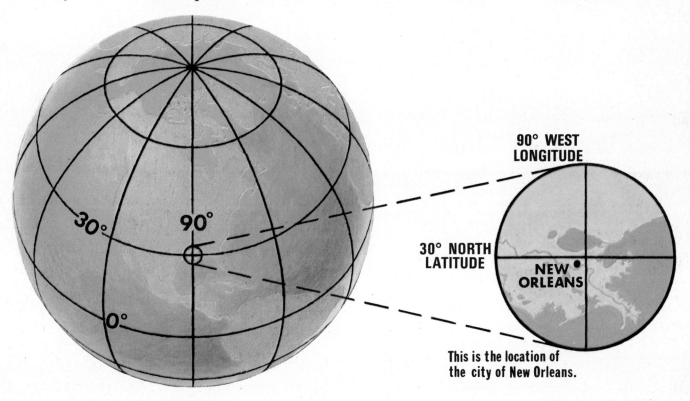

90° WEST LONGITUDE

30° NORTH LATITUDE

NEW ORLEANS

This is the location of the city of New Orleans.

If you know the latitude and longitude of the city of New Orleans, Louisiana, you can locate this city on the earth's grid. On a globe, find the line of latitude numbered 30° North. Then find the line of longitude numbered 90° West. Near the point where these two lines cross each other, you will be able to see the city of New Orleans. This same grid system is also used on maps.

Do you know the latitude and longitude of the town or city where you live?

HOW TO USE A MAP INDEX

BY USING GRID SQUARES

A MAP INDEX is an alphabetical listing of the place names that are on a map. An index will help you find the location of a particular place or point of interest on a map. Suppose you wanted to find the location of Philadelphia, Pennsylvania. Look at the index below the map at the right. You find "Philadelphia, C2." At the top of the map, find the letter C. Along the side of the map, find the number 2. Follow the shaded row down from the letter C. Find the grid square where it meets the shaded row running across from the number 2. Here you find the name Philadelphia.

INDEX

Annapolis .... B 4
Baltimore .... B 3
Harrisburg .... B 2
New York .... E 2
Philadelphia .... C 2 ◄
Washington .... A 4

BY USING LATITUDE AND LONGITUDE

Some indexes give degrees of latitude and longitude. These can also help you locate places on a map or globe. Remember, the east-west horizontal lines describe the degrees (°) and minutes (') of latitude. There are 60 minutes in each degree. The north-south vertical lines describe the degrees and minutes of longitude. Look at the index below the map. You find "Philadelphia, 40°00'N, 75°10'W." This means that Philadelphia is located at 40°00' North Latitude, 75°10' West Longitude. On the map find the 40° horizontal line. Next, find the 75°10' vertical line. This line is a bit west of the line marked 75°. Where these two lines cross, you find the city symbol for Philadelphia.

INDEX

Annapolis .... 38°59'N. 76°30'W.
Baltimore .... 39°17'N. 76°37'W.
Harrisburg .... 40°16'N. 76°53'W.
New York .... 40°43'N. 74°00'W.
Philadelphia ...... 40°00'N. 75°10'W. ◄
Washington .... 38°54'N. 77°02'W.

MAP PROJECTIONS

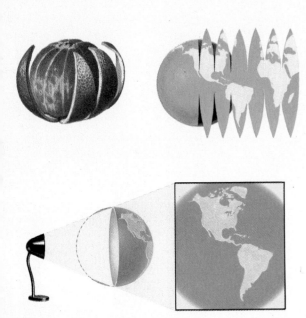

Mapmakers have a problem when they try to show our round earth on a map which is flat. Flat maps always stretch, or distort, some part of the earth's surface. You can "peel" a globe as you can peel an orange. But an interrupted map made from this "peeling" is difficult to use.

A better way to make a map is to PROJECT the features of the round globe onto a flat surface. There are many kinds of PROJECTIONS. Each kind shows at least one area of the earth accurately. But other areas will be distorted. Look at the different projections shown below. The land areas are shown accurately on the interrupted map, but the water areas are broken apart. On the Mercator map, see how some land and water areas are stretched out of shape.

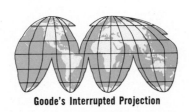

Goode's Interrupted Projection

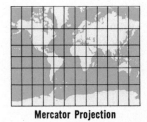

Mercator Projection

TIME ZONES

The measurement of time is very necessary to the daily activities of our lives. It is important that we be at school on time. Airplanes, trains, and buses must maintain definite time schedules. Television programs start at a definite time. Can you imagine all the problems we would have if there were no way of measuring time exactly?

One way of measuring time is by the sun. The sun appears to rise in the east, travel across the sky during the day, and finally set in the west. This apparent movement of the sun is caused by the earth's rotation. Remember, when our part of the earth faces the sun, it is daytime. When our part of the earth turns away from the sun, it is nighttime.

When it is 9 A.M. on the east coast of the United States, a student would be in school. On the west coast, where it is only 6 A.M., a student may still be sleeping.

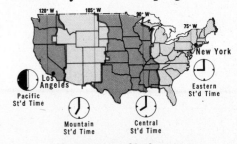

See page 62 for map of World Time Zones.

160° A 140° B 120° C 100° D 80° E 60° F 40° G 20° H 0°

1

ARCTIC OCEAN

80°

GREENLAND

2

ICELAND

Arctic Circle

U.S.
ALASKA

NORTH

60°

UNITED
KINGDOM

CANADA

IRELAND

3

E

AMERICA

FRANC

40°

UNITED STATES

SPAIN

PORTUGAL

ATLANTIC

MOROCCO

4

ALGER

North Tropic Line (Tropic of Cancer)

20°

U.S.
HAWAII

MEXICO

WEST

MAURITANIA

A

5

INDIES

PACIFIC

CENTRAL
AMERICA

VENEZUELA

Equator

COLOMBIA

NIGER

0°

SOUTH

6

PERU

BRAZIL

OCEAN

AMERICA

20°

South Tropic Line (Tropic of Capricorn)

7

OCEAN

CHILE

ARGENTINA

40°

N

W   E

8

WEST LONGITUDE

PRIME MERIDIAN

S

60°

Antarctic Circle

9

ANTARCTICA

160° A 140° B 120° C 100° D 80° E 60° F 40° G 20° H 0°

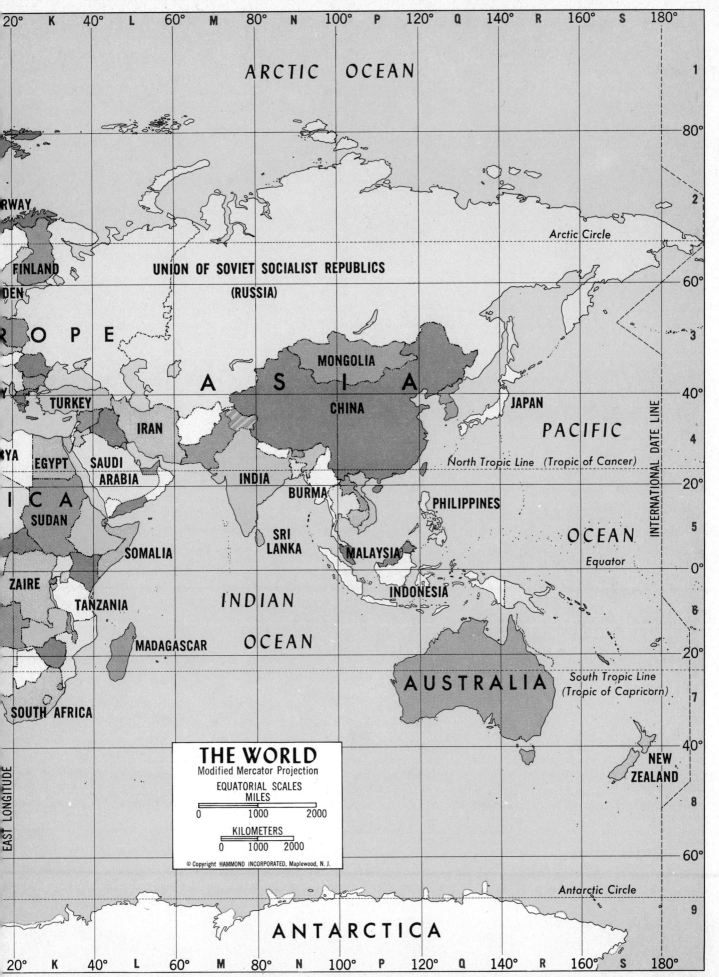

ARCTIC OCEAN

1

80°

2

Arctic Circle

RWAY

FINLAND

DEN

UNION OF SOVIET SOCIALIST REPUBLICS

(RUSSIA)

60°

ROPE

3

ASIA

MONGOLIA

40°

TURKEY

CHINA

JAPAN

PACIFIC

4

IRAN

YA

EGYPT

SAUDI
ARABIA

North Tropic Line (Tropic of Cancer)

20°

ICA

INDIA

SUDAN

BURMA

PHILIPPINES

OCEAN

5

SRI
LANKA

SOMALIA

MALAYSIA

Equator

0°

ZAIRE

INDONESIA

6

TANZANIA

INDIAN

MADAGASCAR

OCEAN

20°

SOUTH AFRICA

AUSTRALIA

South Tropic Line
(Tropic of Capricorn)

7

40°

NEW
ZEALAND

EAST LONGITUDE

THE WORLD
Modified Mercator Projection
EQUATORIAL SCALES
MILES

0   1000   2000

KILOMETERS

0   1000   2000

© Copyright HAMMOND INCORPORATED, Maplewood, N.J.

8

60°

Antarctic Circle

9

ANTARCTICA

INTERNATIONAL DATE LINE

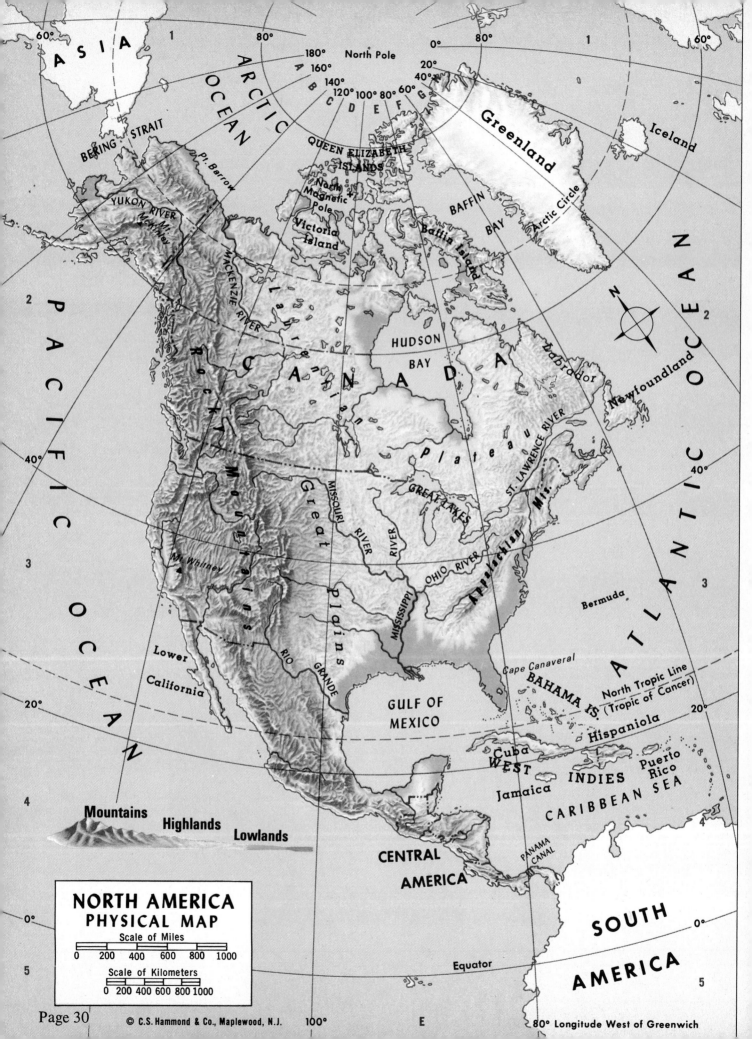

ASIA

ARCTIC OCEAN

BERING STRAIT

Pt. Barrow

North Pole

180°
160°
140°
120° 100° 80° 60°

QUEEN ELIZABETH ISLANDS

Greenland

Iceland

60°
80°
0°
20°
40°

YUKON RIVER
Mt. McKinley

MACKENZIE RIVER

North Magnetic Pole

Victoria Island

BAFFIN BAY

Baffin Island

Arctic Circle

PACIFIC OCEAN

2

CANADA

HUDSON BAY

Labrador

Newfoundland

N

ATLANTIC OCEAN

2

40°

Rocky Mountains

Plateau

GREAT LAKES

ST. LAWRENCE RIVER

Appalachian Mts.

40°

3

Mt. Whitney

Great Plains

MISSOURI RIVER

RIVER

OHIO RIVER

MISSISSIPPI

Bermuda

ATLANTIC OCEAN

3

PACIFIC OCEAN

Lower California

RIO GRANDE

Cape Canaveral

BAHAMA IS.

North Tropic Line
(Tropic of Cancer)

20°

GULF OF MEXICO

Hispaniola

20°

Cuba

WEST INDIES

Puerto Rico

Jamaica

CARIBBEAN SEA

4

Mountains

Highlands

Lowlands

CENTRAL AMERICA

PANAMA CANAL

4

NORTH AMERICA
PHYSICAL MAP

Scale of Miles

0 200 400 600 800 1000

Scale of Kilometers

0 200 400 600 800 1000

SOUTH AMERICA

0°

0°

5

Equator

5

© C.S. Hammond & Co., Maplewood, N.J.

100°

E

80° Longitude West of Greenwich

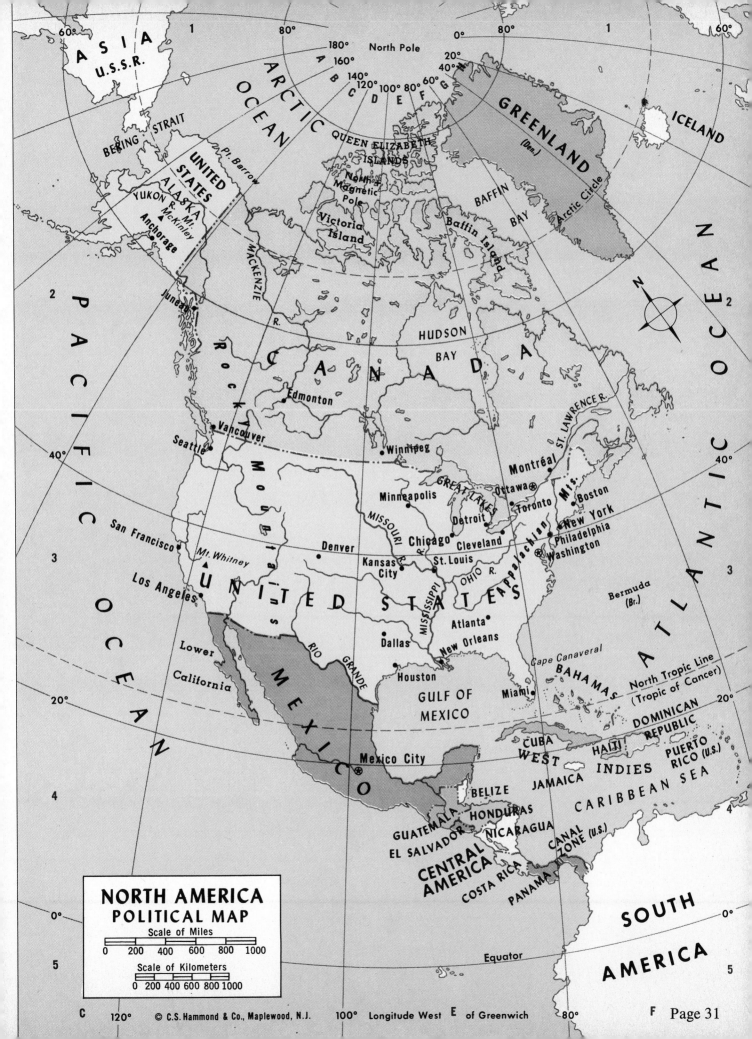

ASIA
U.S.S.R.

ARCTIC OCEAN

North Pole

GREENLAND
(Den.)

ICELAND

BERING STRAIT

QUEEN ELIZABETH ISLANDS

Pt. Barrow

UNITED STATES
ALASKA
YUKON R.
Mt. McKinley
Anchorage

North Magnetic Pole

Victoria Island

Baffin Island

BAFFIN BAY

Arctic Circle

MACKENZIE

Juneau

R.

CANADA

HUDSON BAY

ST. LAWRENCE R.

PACIFIC OCEAN

ATLANTIC OCEAN

ROCKY Mountains

Edmonton

Vancouver
Seattle

Winnipeg

Montréal
Ottawa
Toronto
Boston

San Francisco

Minneapolis

MISSOURI R.

GREAT LAKES

Detroit

New York
Philadelphia

Mt. Whitney

Denver

Kansas City

Chicago
St. Louis
Cleveland
OHIO R.
Appalachian Mts.
Washington

Los Angeles

UNITED STATES

MISSISSIPPI R.

Atlanta

Bermuda (Br.)

Lower California

RIO GRANDE

Dallas

New Orleans

Cape Canaveral

MEXICO

Houston

GULF OF MEXICO

Miami

BAHAMAS

North Tropic Line
(Tropic of Cancer)

CUBA

WEST INDIES

HAITI

DOMINICAN REPUBLIC

PUERTO RICO (U.S.)

Mexico City

JAMAICA

CARIBBEAN SEA

BELIZE

GUATEMALA
EL SALVADOR

HONDURAS
NICARAGUA

CENTRAL AMERICA

COSTA RICA

PANAMA

CANAL ZONE (U.S.)

SOUTH AMERICA

Equator

NORTH AMERICA
POLITICAL MAP

Scale of Miles
0   200   400   600   800   1000

Scale of Kilometers
0   200 400 600 800 1000

© C.S. Hammond & Co., Maplewood, N.J.   Longitude West of Greenwich   Page 31

NORTH AMERICA   VEGETATION

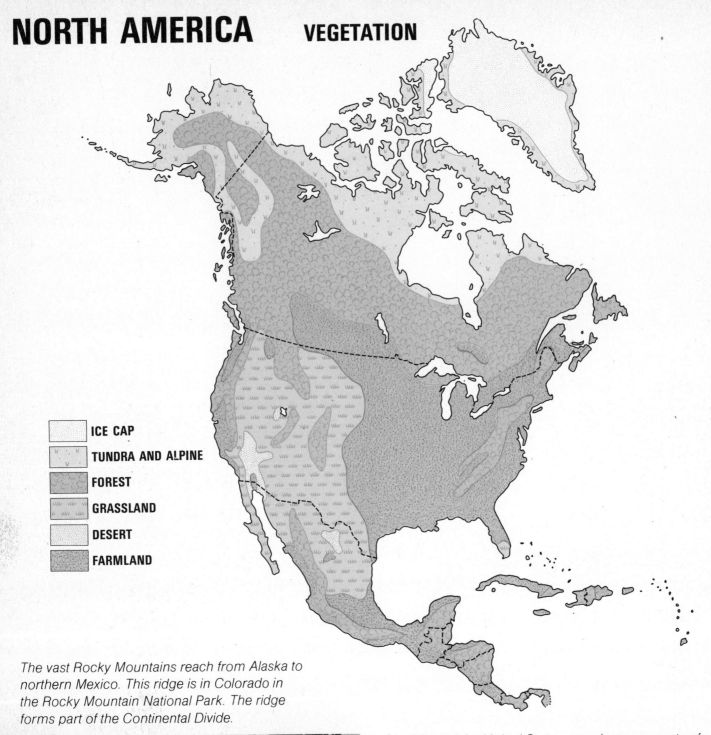

ICE CAP

TUNDRA AND ALPINE

FOREST

GRASSLAND

DESERT

FARMLAND

The vast Rocky Mountains reach from Alaska to northern Mexico. This ridge is in Colorado in the Rocky Mountain National Park. The ridge forms part of the Continental Divide.

Canada and the United States grow large amounts of wheat. Some of it is exported to other countries. These combines are harvesting wheat grown in Canada.

POPULATION

- ▉ VERY CROWDED LANDS
- ▉ CROWDED LANDS
- ▉ LESS CROWDED LANDS
- ▉ ALMOST EMPTY LANDS
- ▉ LANDS WHERE NO ONE LIVES

LEADING PRODUCTS

OIL

TIMBER

URANIUM

LEAD & ZINC   OIL

OATS & BARLEY

IRON

FISH

WHEAT

NICKEL & COPPER

TIMBER

IRON

FISH

CORN

HOGS

VEGETABLES

URANIUM

COAL

FRUIT

WHEAT

LEAD

TOBACCO

COPPER

COTTON

CATTLE   OIL

CITRUS FRUIT

LEAD, ZINC & SILVER

SUGARCANE

SUGARCANE

CORN   OIL

BANANAS

BAUXITE

The United States has many big, busy cities with very tall buildings. This is a night view of the skyline of Houston, Texas.

Mexicans gather at a famous church to celebrate a religious holiday. Mexican people enjoy many fiestas (festivals) during the year.

This sunny marketplace is in Pointe-à-Pitre, Guadeloupe. Guadeloupe is an island in the West Indies. Many tourists visit these islands.

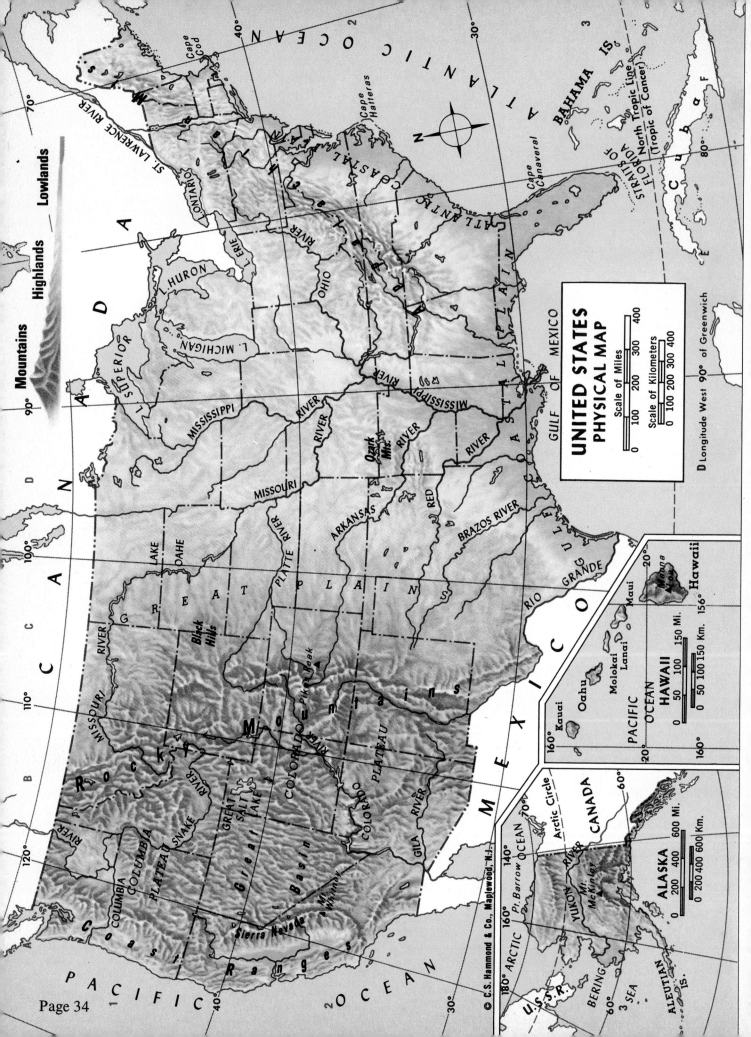

Page 34

Mountains
Highlands
Lowlands

UNITED STATES PHYSICAL MAP

Scale of Miles
0   100   200   300   400

Scale of Kilometers
0   100   200   300   400

D Longitude West 90° of Greenwich

HAWAII
PACIFIC OCEAN
Kauai
Oahu
Molokai
Maui
Lanai
Mauna Loa
Hawaii
Scale of Miles
0   50   100   150 Mi.
0   50 100 150 Km.

ALASKA
ARCTIC OCEAN
Pt. Barrow
Arctic Circle
CANADA
Yukon River
Mt. McKinley
BERING SEA
ALEUTIAN IS.
U.S.S.R.
0   200   400   600 Mi.
0   200 400 600 Km.

CANADA

PACIFIC OCEAN

ATLANTIC OCEAN

GULF OF MEXICO

MEXICO

Cape Cod
Cape Hatteras
Cape Canaveral
BAHAMA IS.
STRAITS OF FLORIDA
North Tropic line
(Tropic of Cancer)
Cuba

ST. LAWRENCE RIVER
L. ONTARIO
L. ERIE
L. HURON
L. MICHIGAN
L. SUPERIOR

ATLANTIC COASTAL PLAIN
GULF COASTAL PLAIN

OHIO RIVER
MISSISSIPPI RIVER
MISSOURI RIVER
PLATTE RIVER
ARKANSAS RIVER
RED RIVER
BRAZOS RIVER
RIO GRANDE
COLORADO RIVER
GILA RIVER
SNAKE RIVER
COLUMBIA RIVER
MISSOURI RIVER

Ozark Mts.
GREAT PLAINS
Black Hills
Pikes Peak
Rocky Mountains
COLORADO PLATEAU
GREAT SALT LAKE
Great Basin
LAKE OAHE
COLUMBIA PLATEAU
Sierra Nevada
Mt. Whitney
Coast Ranges

© C.S. Hammond & Co., Maplewood, N.J.

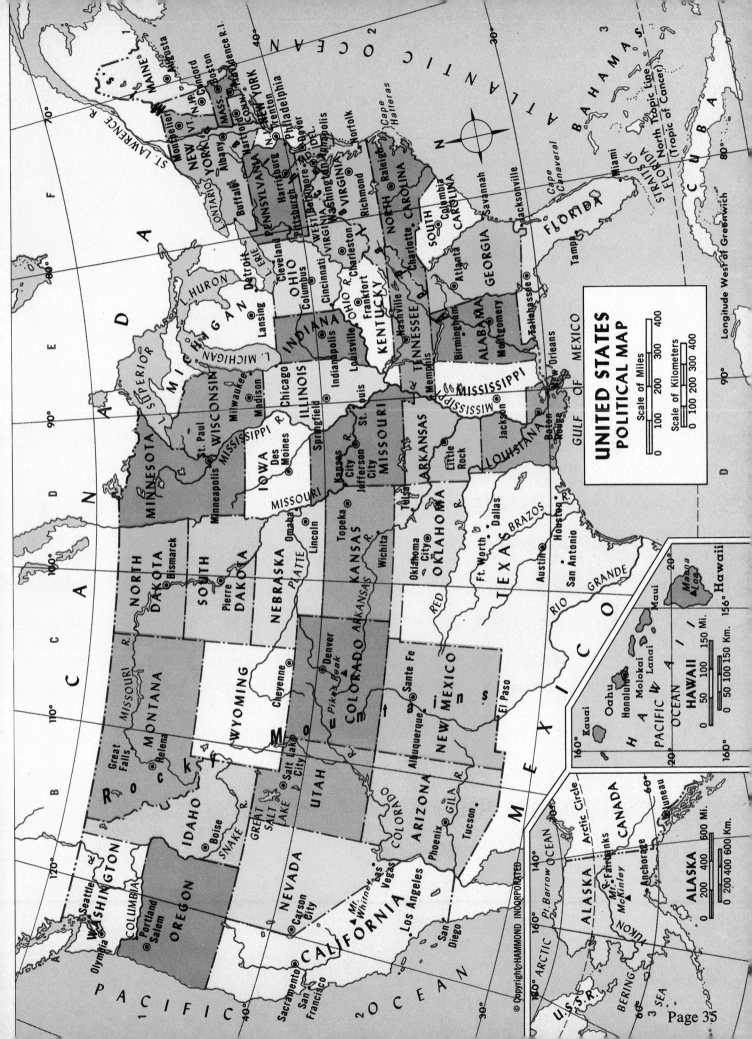

UNITED STATES
POLITICAL MAP

Scale of Miles
0   100   200   300   400

Scale of Kilometers
0   100   200   300   400

© Copyright HAMMOND INCORPORATED

Page 35

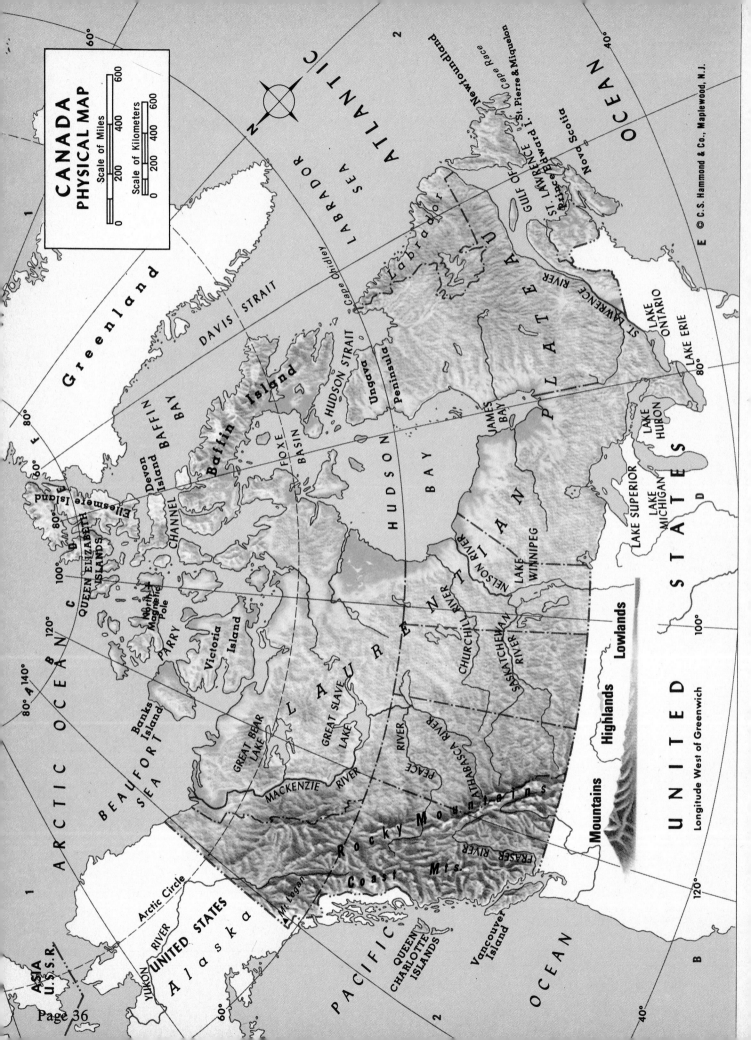

CANADA
PHYSICAL MAP

Scale of Miles
0   200   400   600

Scale of Kilometers
0   200   400   600

© C.S. Hammond & Co., Maplewood, N.J.

ASIA
U.S.S.R.

ARCTIC OCEAN

BEAUFORT SEA

Banks Island

North Magnetic Pole

Queen Elizabeth Islands

Ellesmere Island

Greenland

Devon Island

BAFFIN BAY

DAVIS STRAIT

Baffin Island

PARRY CHANNEL

Victoria Island

FOXE BASIN

HUDSON STRAIT

Ungava Peninsula

LABRADOR SEA

ATLANTIC OCEAN

Cape Chidley

Labrador

Newfoundland

Cape Race

St. Pierre & Miquelon

GULF OF ST. LAWRENCE

Prince Edward I.

Nova Scotia

ST. LAWRENCE RIVER

LAKE ONTARIO

LAKE ERIE

LAKE HURON

LAKE SUPERIOR

LAKE MICHIGAN

HUDSON BAY

JAMES BAY

LAURENTIAN PLATEAU

NELSON RIVER

LAKE WINNIPEG

CHURCHILL RIVER

SASKATCHEWAN RIVER

ATHABASCA RIVER

PEACE RIVER

Great Bear Lake

Great Slave Lake

MACKENZIE RIVER

Rocky Mountains

Coast Mts.

Mt. Logan

Arctic Circle

YUKON RIVER

UNITED STATES
Alaska

FRASER RIVER

PACIFIC OCEAN

Queen Charlotte Islands

Vancouver Island

UNITED STATES

Longitude West of Greenwich

Mountains   Highlands   Lowlands

80°   60°   40°

100°   120°   140°

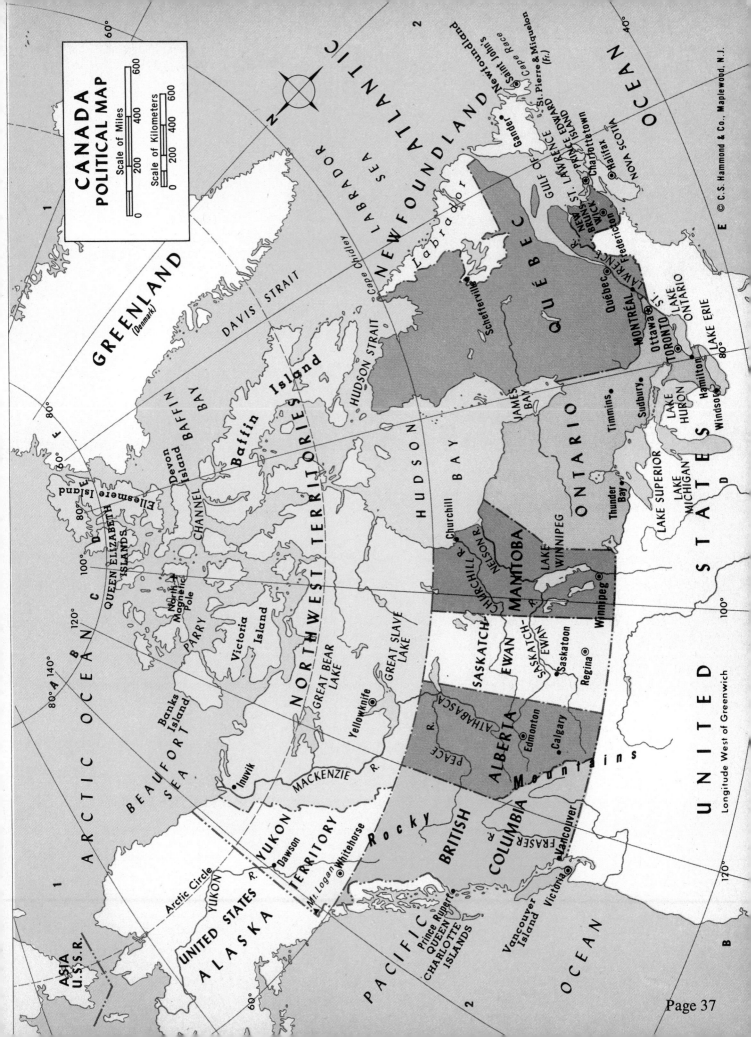

A 80° CARIBBEAN B SEA WEST 60° INDIES C 40° D

CENTRAL
AMERICA

Punta Gallinas

ATLANTIC

OCEAN

1   1

ORINOCO
RIVER

Llanos

Guiana   Highlands

Equator

0°   0°

RIO   NEGRO   AMAZON RIVER

Cabo de
São Roque

AMAZON   RIVER

S e l v a s   RIO MADEIRA   RIO TAPAJOS

Caatingas

Andes

2   2

LAKE
TITICACA

Mato Grosso
Plateau

TOCANTINS   RIO   SÃO FRANCISCO   Campos

Brazilian

Mountains

Gran Chaco

Highlands

20°   20°

South Tropic Line
(Tropic of Capricorn)

PARANÁ

PACIFIC

Pampas

RIO

RIO URUGUAY

N

3   3

Aconcagua

RIO DE LA PLATA

OCEAN

ATLANTIC OCEAN

Patagonia

SOUTH AMERICA
PHYSICAL MAP

Scale of Miles

0   200   400   600   800

Scale of Kilometers

0   200   400   600   800

40°   40°

FALKLAND
ISLANDS

Mountains

Highlands

Lowlands

STRAIT OF
MAGELLAN

Tierra del
Fuego

4   4

© C.S. Hammond & Co., Maplewood, N.J.

Cape Horn

Page 38   A   80°   B   60°   C Longitude West 40° of Greenwich D   20°

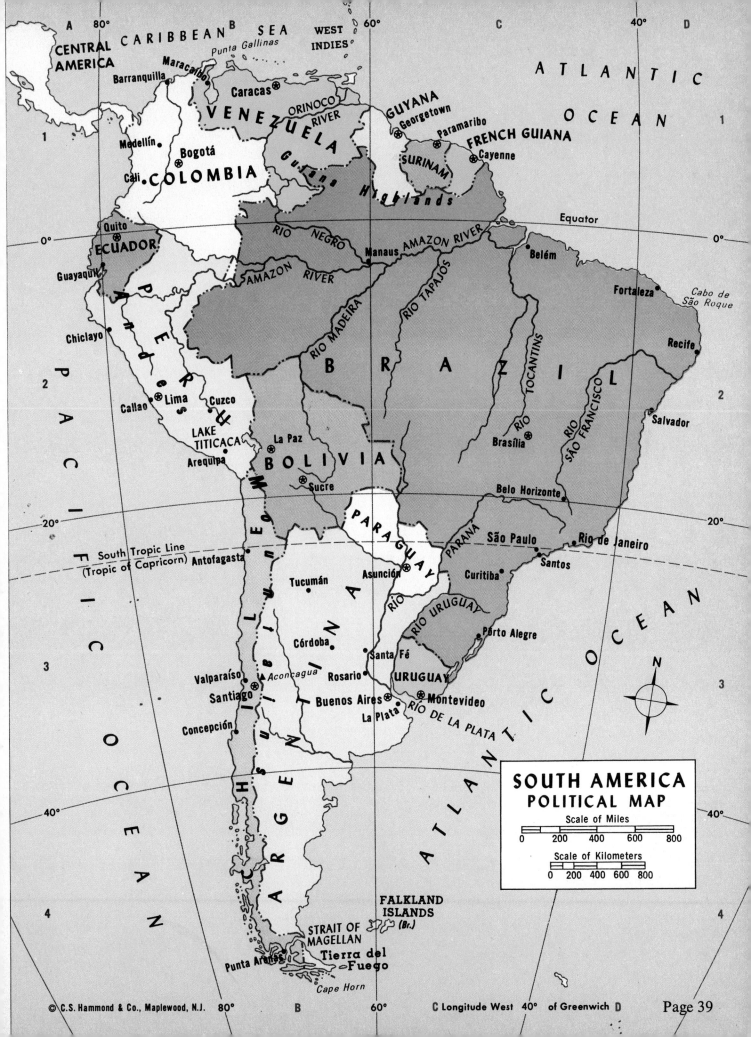

CENTRAL AMERICA

CARIBBEAN

Punta Gallinas

WEST INDIES

ATLANTIC

OCEAN

Maracaibo

Barranquilla

Caracas ⊛

VENEZUELA

ORINOCO RIVER

GUYANA

Georgetown •

Paramaribo •

FRENCH GUIANA

1

Medellín •

Bogotá ⊛

COLOMBIA

Guiana

SURINAM

Cayenne ⊛

Cali •

Highlands

Equator

Quito ⊛

ECUADOR

0°

RIO NEGRO

Manaus • AMAZON RIVER

Belém •

0°

Guayaquil •

AMAZON RIVER

RIO TAPAJOS

Chiclayo •

A

n

d

e

P

E

R

U

RIO MADEIRA

B   R   A   Z   I   L

RIO TOCANTINS

Fortaleza •

*Cabo de
São Roque*

Recife •

Callao ⊛ Lima

Cuzco •

s

RIO SÃO FRANCISCO

2

LAKE
TITICACA

La Paz •

Brasília ⊛

RIO

Salvador •

2

Arequipa •

BOLIVIA

Sucre ⊛

Belo Horizonte •

South Tropic Line
(Tropic of Capricorn)

Antofagasta •

PARAGUAY

São Paulo •

Rio de Janeiro •

20°

20°

M
e
n
d
o
z
a

Tucumán •

Asunción ⊛

PARANA

Santos •

Curitiba •

Córdoba •

A R G E N T I N A

RIO

RIO URUGUAY

Pôrto Alegre •

3

Valparaíso •

Aconcagua

Rosario •

Santa Fé •

URUGUAY

PACIFIC OCEAN

ATLANTIC OCEAN

N

3

Santiago ⊛

Buenos Aires ⊛

⊛ Montevideo

La Plata •

RIO DE LA PLATA

Concepción •

C
h
i
l
e

FALKLAND
ISLANDS
(Br.)

SOUTH AMERICA
POLITICAL MAP

Scale of Miles

| 0 | 200 | 400 | 600 | 800 |

Scale of Kilometers

| 0 | 200 | 400 | 600 | 800 |

4

STRAIT OF
MAGELLAN

Punta Arenas •

Tierra del
Fuego

Cape Horn

4

80° B 60° C Longitude West 40° of Greenwich D

SOUTH AMERICA VEGETATION

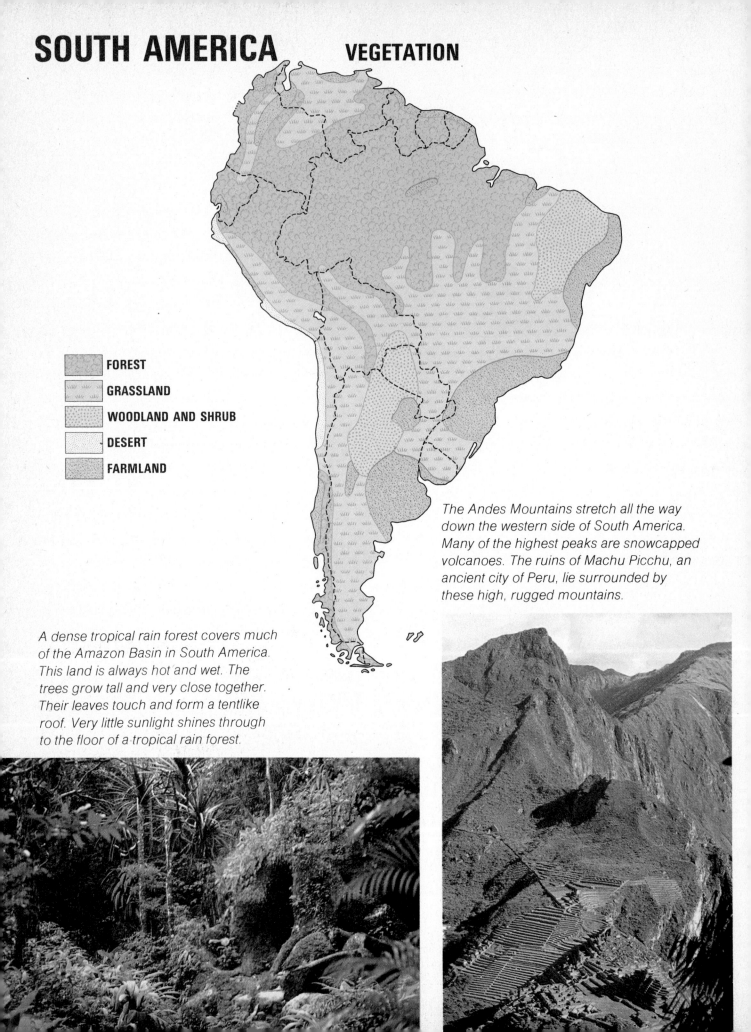

FOREST

GRASSLAND

WOODLAND AND SHRUB

DESERT

FARMLAND

The Andes Mountains stretch all the way down the western side of South America. Many of the highest peaks are snowcapped volcanoes. The ruins of Machu Picchu, an ancient city of Peru, lie surrounded by these high, rugged mountains.

A dense tropical rain forest covers much of the Amazon Basin in South America. This land is always hot and wet. The trees grow tall and very close together. Their leaves touch and form a tentlike roof. Very little sunlight shines through to the floor of a tropical rain forest.

POPULATION

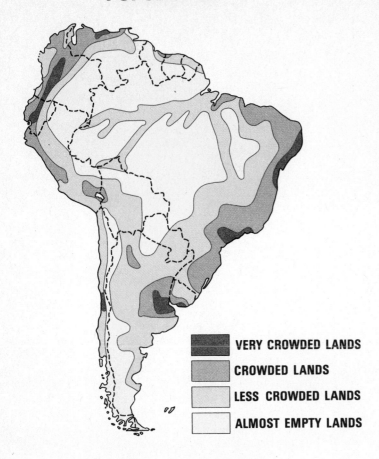

VERY CROWDED LANDS

CROWDED LANDS

LESS CROWDED LANDS

ALMOST EMPTY LANDS

LEADING PRODUCTS

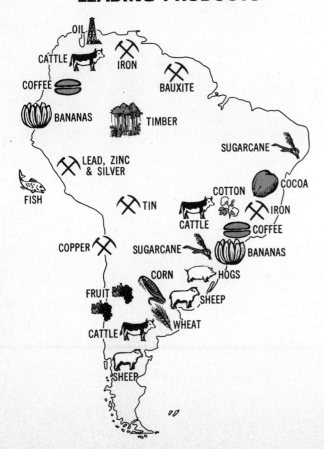

OIL
CATTLE
IRON
COFFEE
BAUXITE
BANANAS
TIMBER
SUGARCANE
LEAD, ZINC & SILVER
COCOA
FISH
COTTON
IRON
TIN
CATTLE
COFFEE
COPPER
SUGARCANE
BANANAS
CORN
HOGS
FRUIT
SHEEP
CATTLE
WHEAT
SHEEP

Peruvian women display their handicrafts in an open marketplace. The women are dressed in native Indian style.

There are many rich mineral deposits in South America. This open-pit copper mine is in Chile. Find out what copper is used for.

Coffee berries are picked by hand when they turn bright red. Inside each berry are two coffee beans. The beans must be dried and roasted before using. Brazil and Colombia are the leading coffee-producing nations.

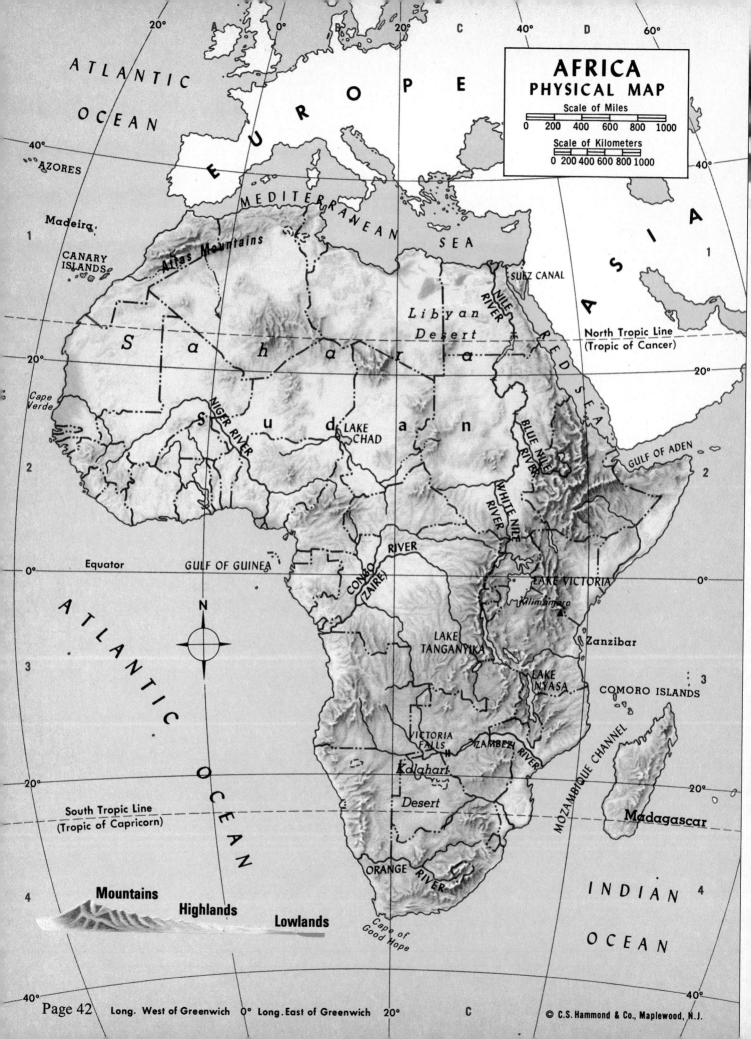

AFRICA
PHYSICAL MAP

Scale of Miles

0 200 400 600 800 1000

Scale of Kilometers

0 200 400 600 800 1000

ATLANTIC OCEAN

EUROPE

ASIA

AZORES

Madeira

CANARY ISLANDS

MEDITERRANEAN SEA

Atlas Mountains

Cape Verde

S a h a r a

Libyan Desert

SUEZ CANAL

NILE RIVER

RED SEA

North Tropic Line (Tropic of Cancer)

S u d a n

NIGER RIVER

LAKE CHAD

BLUE NILE RIVER

WHITE NILE RIVER

GULF OF ADEN

Equator

GULF OF GUINEA

CONGO (ZAIRE) RIVER

LAKE VICTORIA

Kilimanjaro

Zanzibar

ATLANTIC OCEAN

N

LAKE TANGANYIKA

LAKE NYASA

COMORO ISLANDS

VICTORIA FALLS

ZAMBEZI RIVER

Kalahari Desert

MOZAMBIQUE CHANNEL

Madagascar

South Tropic Line (Tropic of Capricorn)

ORANGE RIVER

Cape of Good Hope

INDIAN OCEAN

Mountains

Highlands

Lowlands

Long. West of Greenwich 0° Long. East of Greenwich 20°

AFRICA

VEGETATION

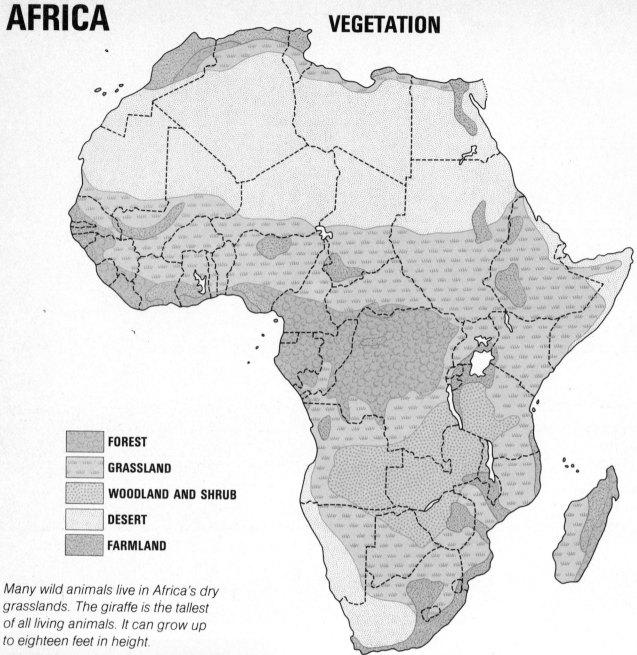

- FOREST
- GRASSLAND
- WOODLAND AND SHRUB
- DESERT
- FARMLAND

Many wild animals live in Africa's dry grasslands. The giraffe is the tallest of all living animals. It can grow up to eighteen feet in height.

The Sahara is the largest desert area in the world. Here an Arab rests his camel near the pyramids of Egypt. Why are camels so important for desert travel?

POPULATION

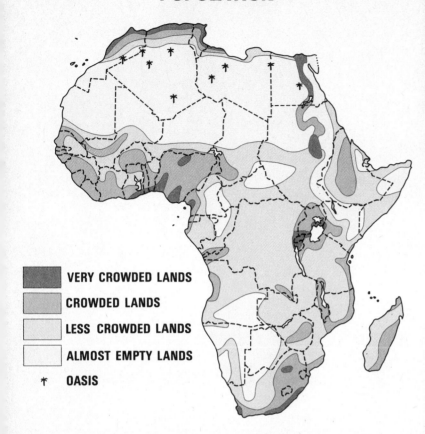

VERY CROWDED LANDS
CROWDED LANDS
LESS CROWDED LANDS
ALMOST EMPTY LANDS
✝ OASIS

LEADING PRODUCTS

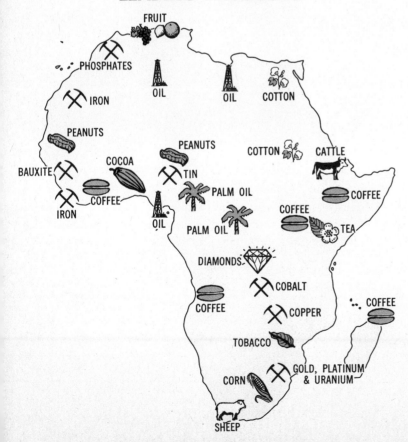

FRUIT
PHOSPHATES
IRON
OIL
OIL
COTTON
PEANUTS
PEANUTS
COTTON
CATTLE
BAUXITE
COCOA
TIN
COFFEE
IRON
COFFEE
OIL
PALM OIL
COFFEE
PALM OIL
TEA
DIAMONDS
COBALT
COFFEE
COPPER
COFFEE
TOBACCO
CORN
GOLD, PLATINUM & URANIUM
SHEEP

Modern apartment buildings rise in a new section of Kinshasa. It is the capital and largest city in Zaire.

Africa's large cities have offices, stores, factories, and buildings. Here policemen stand on duty in a city square.

Farming and ranching produce much of Kenya's wealth. Cattle can graze on Kenya's high open plains. But most farms are small.

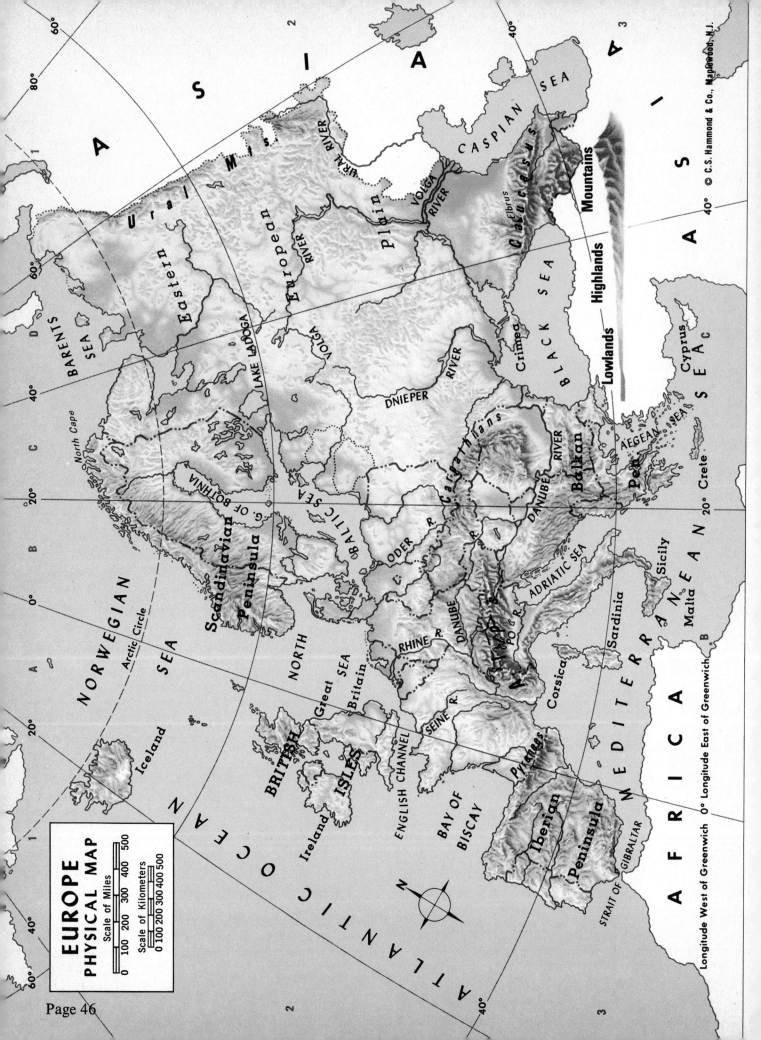

EUROPE
PHYSICAL MAP

Scale of Miles
0 100 200 300 400 500

Scale of Kilometers
0 100 200 300 400 500

A S I A

A S I A

Mountains
Highlands
Lowlands

CASPIAN SEA

Caucasus Mts.
Elbrus

BLACK SEA

Crimea

BARENTS SEA

Ural Mts.

Eastern European Plain

URAL RIVER

VOLGA RIVER

VOLGA RIVER

VOLGA

LAKE LADOGA

DNIEPER RIVER

North Cape

Arctic Circle

NORWEGIAN SEA

Iceland

Scandinavian Peninsula

G. OF BOTHNIA

BALTIC SEA

NORTH SEA

BRITISH ISLES

Great Britain

Ireland

ENGLISH CHANNEL

SEINE R.

BAY OF BISCAY

RHINE R.

ODER R.

ELBE R.

DANUBE

DANUBE RIVER

Carpathians

Balkan

Pen.

AEGEAN SEA

ALPS

PO R.

ADRIATIC SEA

Corsica

Sardinia

Sicily

Malta

MEDITERRANEAN SEA

Pyrenees

Iberian Peninsula

STRAIT OF GIBRALTAR

AFRICA

CYPRUS

SEA

Crete

ATLANTIC OCEAN

N

Longitude West of Greenwich 0° Longitude East of Greenwich

© C.S. Hammond & Co., Maplewood, N.J.

Page 46

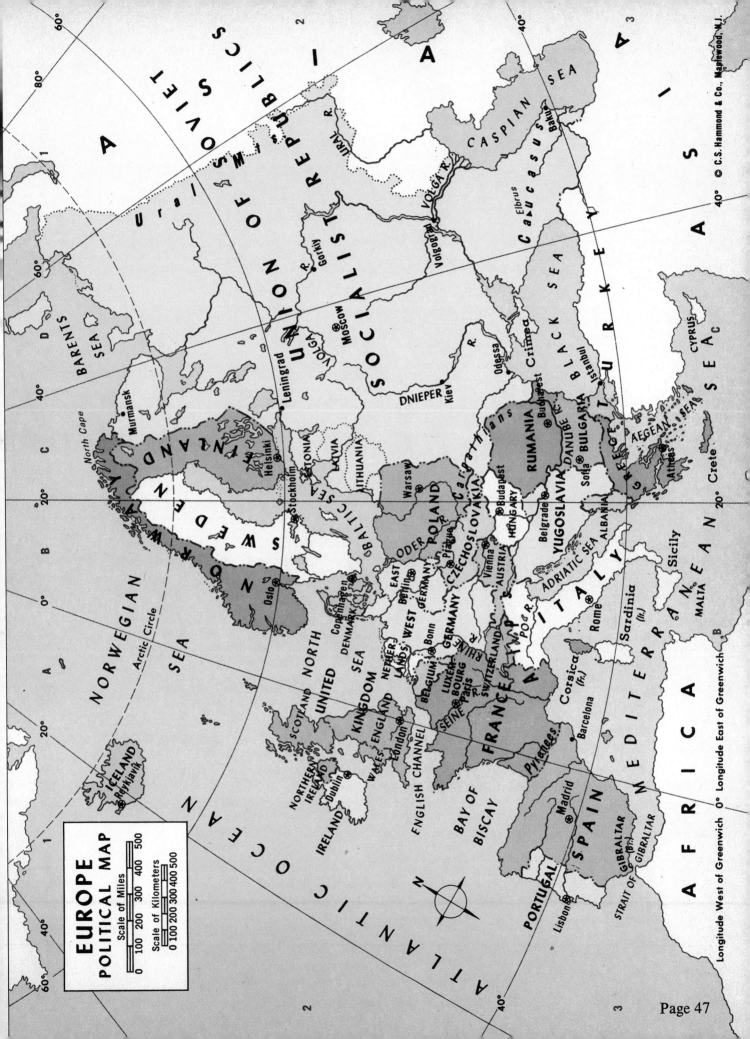

EUROPE
POLITICAL MAP

Scale of Miles
0 100 200 300 400 500

Scale of Kilometers
0 100 200 300 400 500

© C.S. Hammond & Co., Maplewood, N.J.

UNION OF SOVIET SOCIALIST REPUBLICS

BARENTS SEA

NORWEGIAN SEA

North Cape
Murmansk
Ural R.
Gorkiy
Moscow
Volga R.
Ural
VOLGA R.
Volgograd
CASPIAN SEA
Baku
Caucasus
Elbrus

FINLAND
Helsinki
Leningrad
ESTONIA
LATVIA
LITHUANIA
BALTIC SEA
Stockholm
SWEDEN
NORWAY
Oslo

Arctic Circle

DNIEPER
Kiev
Odessa
Crimea
BLACK SEA
Istanbul
TURKEY
CYPRUS
AEGEAN SEA
Athens
Crete
MEDITERRANEAN SEA

Warsaw
POLAND
ODER R.
EAST GERMANY
Berlin
Prague
CZECHOSLOVAKIA
Carpathians
Vienna
AUSTRIA
HUNGARY
Budapest
DANUBE R.
RUMANIA
Bucharest
YUGOSLAVIA
Belgrade
BULGARIA
Sofia
ALBANIA
ADRIATIC SEA
GREECE

Copenhagen
DENMARK
NETHER-LANDS
WEST GERMANY
Bonn
RHINE R.
LUXEMBOURG
BELGIUM
SWITZERLAND
SEINE R.
Paris
FRANCE
PO R.
ITALY
Rome
Corsica (Fr.)
Sardinia (It.)
Sicily
MALTA
Barcelona
Pyrenees
SPAIN
Madrid
PORTUGAL
Lisbon
GIBRALTAR (Br.)
STRAIT OF GIBRALTAR

SCOTLAND
NORTH SEA
UNITED KINGDOM
ENGLAND
London
WALES
NORTHERN IRELAND
Dublin
IRELAND
ENGLISH CHANNEL
BAY OF BISCAY

ICELAND
Reykjavik

ATLANTIC OCEAN

AFRICA

Longitude West of Greenwich   0° Longitude East of Greenwich   20°

EUROPE

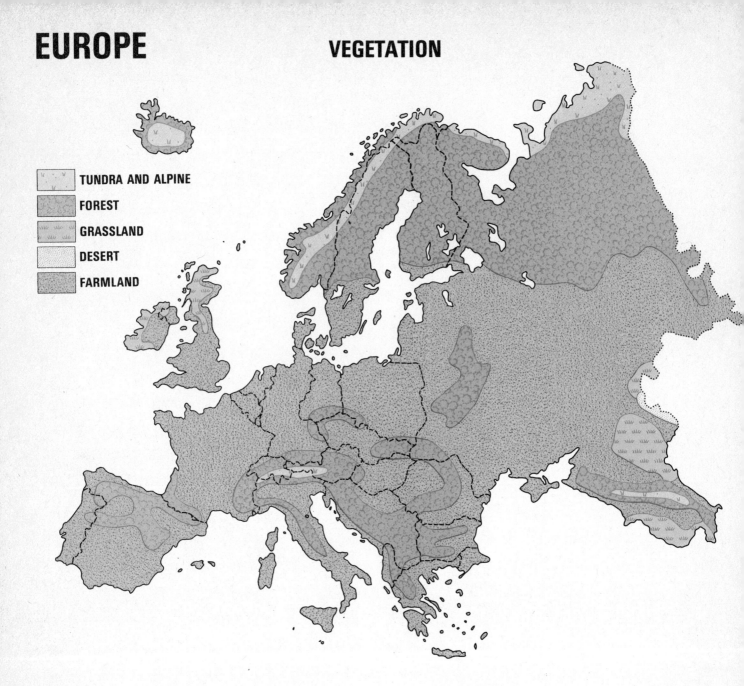

TUNDRA AND ALPINE

FOREST

GRASSLAND

DESERT

FARMLAND

Large ships can travel on many of Europe's rivers and canals. These waterways are an important part of the land's transportation system. Many of the world's major ports are located on these waterways. Products are shipped from these ports to nations all over the world.

Mountain ranges cover much of southern Europe. The Alps are the most famous of these ranges. Winter sports and beautiful scenery attract many tourists.

POPULATION

VERY CROWDED LANDS

CROWDED LANDS

LESS CROWDED LANDS

ALMOST EMPTY LANDS

LEADING PRODUCTS

FISH

IRON

TIMBER

TIMBER

TIMBER

OATS

SHEEP

OIL

OIL

FLAX

RYE

WHEAT

COAL

GAS

POTATOES

SUGAR BEETS

RYE & OATS

CATTLE

WHEAT & BARLEY

FISH

WHEAT

IRON & COAL

COAL

IRON & COAL

SHEEP

OIL

WHEAT

OLIVES

GRAPES

CORN

OIL

FRUIT

CORK

FRUIT

OLIVES

LEAD & ZINC

COTTON

Europe is a small continent with a large population. West Berlin, in Germany, is one of its large cities. How can you tell that it is a big city?

Farmers in France harvest grapes by hand. Some of the world's richest farmland is in Europe. About one-half of the land area is cultivated.

Northern Europe has little good farmland. But its forests are an important resource. These logs are being towed to a sawmill. Lumber, wood pulp, and paper are important products.

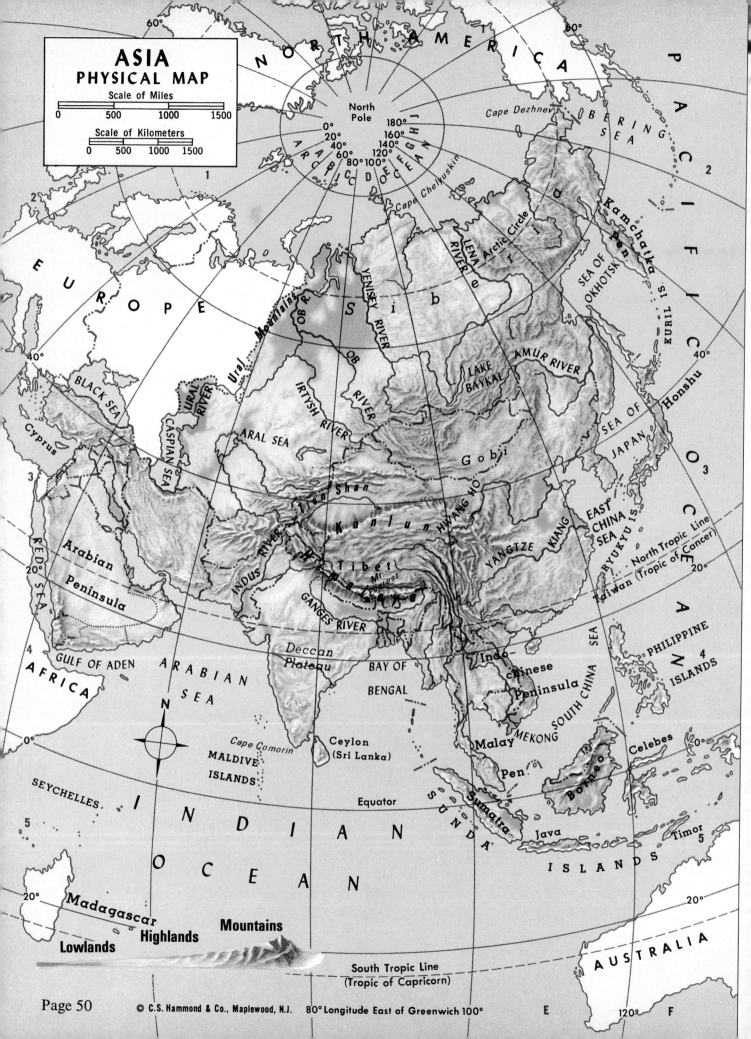

ASIA
PHYSICAL MAP

Scale of Miles

0   500   1000   1500

Scale of Kilometers

0   500   1000   1500

NORTH AMERICA

PACIFIC

60°   80°

North Pole

Cape Dezhnev

BERING SEA

0°
20°
40°
60°
80° 100°
120°
140°
160°
180°

Cape Chelyuskin

ARCTIC OCEAN

LENA RIVER

Arctic Circle

SEA OF OKHOTSK

Kamchatka Pen.

KURIL IS.

EUROPE

Ural Mountains

OB R.

YENISEY RIVER

S i b e r i a

LAKE BAYKAL

AMUR RIVER

SEA OF JAPAN

Honshu

40°   40°

BLACK SEA

URAL RIVER

Ural River

IRTYSH RIVER

OB RIVER

Gobi

HWANG HO

PACIFIC OCEAN

Cyprus

CASPIAN SEA

ARAL SEA

Tien Shan

K u n l u n

YANGTZE

KIANG

EAST CHINA SEA

RYUKYU IS.

3   3

Arabian Peninsula

INDUS RIVER

H i m a l a y a

Tibet

Mt. Everest

North Tropic Line
(Tropic of Cancer)

Taiwan (Tropic of Cancer)

20°   20°

RED SEA

GANGES RIVER

Deccan Plateau

BAY OF BENGAL

Indo-chinese Peninsula

PHILIPPINE ISLANDS

GULF OF ADEN

ARABIAN SEA

N

SOUTH CHINA SEA

4   4

AFRICA

Cape Comorin

Ceylon (Sri Lanka)

MALDIVE ISLANDS

Malay Pen.

MEKONG

Celebes

0°   0°

SEYCHELLES

Equator

SUNDA

Sumatra

Borneo

Java

Timor

ISLANDS

INDIAN OCEAN

5   5

20°   20°

Madagascar

Mountains

Highlands

Lowlands

South Tropic Line
(Tropic of Capricorn)

AUSTRALIA

120°

Page 50   © C.S. Hammond & Co., Maplewood, N.J.   80° Longitude East of Greenwich 100°

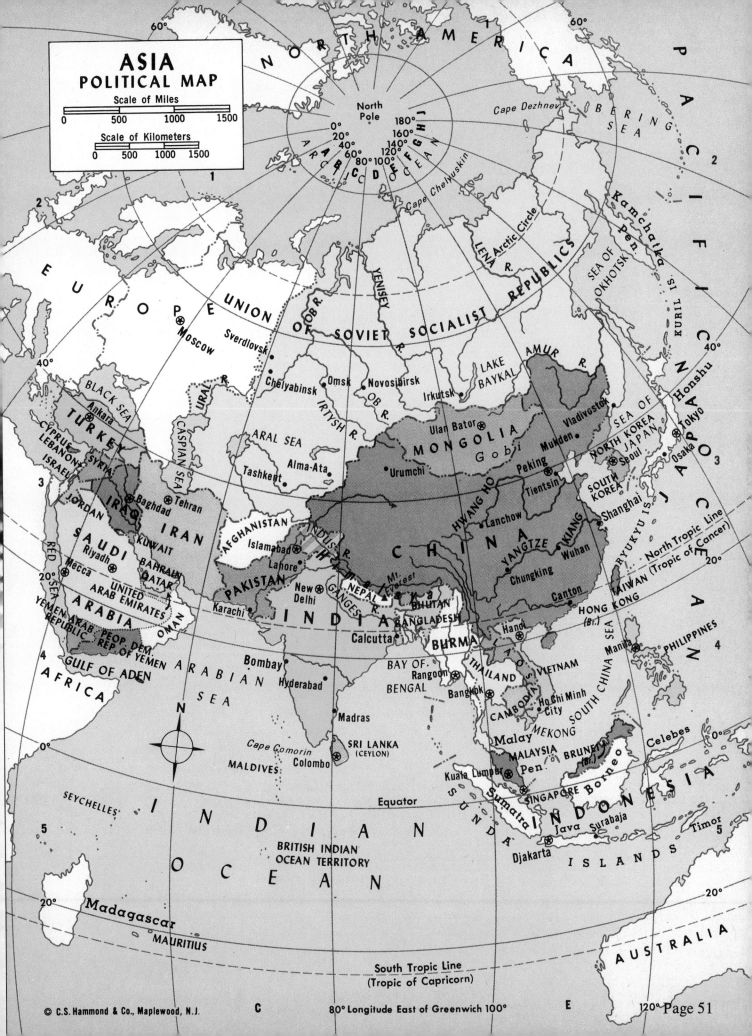

ASIA
POLITICAL MAP
Scale of Miles

0   500   1000   1500

Scale of Kilometers

0   500   1000   1500

NORTH AMERICA

PACIFIC

North Pole

Cape Dezhnev

BERING SEA

Cape Chelyuskin

Arctic Circle

KURIL IS.

LENA R.

Kamchatka Pen.

SEA OF OKHOTSK

EUROPE

UNION

OB R.

SOVIET SOCIALIST REPUBLICS

Moscow

Sverdlovsk

YENISEY

LAKE BAYKAL

AMUR R.

Chelyabinsk   Omsk   Novosibirsk

Irkutsk

OB R.

Vladivostok

SEA OF JAPAN

Honshu

Tokyo

BLACK SEA

Ankara

URAL R.

ARAL SEA

IRTYSH R.

Ulan Bator

MONGOLIA

Gobi

Mukden

NORTH KOREA

TURKEY

CASPIAN SEA

Alma-Ata

Urumchi

Peking

Tientsin

Seoul

SOUTH KOREA

Osaka

JAPAN

CYPRUS

LEBANON

SYRIA

ISRAEL

JORDAN

IRAQ

Baghdad   Tehran

IRAN

Tashkent

AFGHANISTAN

HWANG HO

Lanchow

CHINA

Shanghai

RYUKYU IS.

North Tropic Line
(Tropic of Cancer)

SAUDI

KUWAIT

Riyadh

BAHRAIN

QATAR

Islamabad

INDUS R.

YANGTZE

KIANG

Wuhan

Chungking

RED SEA

Mecca

UNITED ARAB EMIRATES

Lahore

PAKISTAN

NEPAL

Mt. Everest

BHUTAN

Canton

HONG KONG
(Br.)

TAIWAN

YEMEN ARAB REPUBLIC

ARABIA

PEOP. DEM. REP. OF YEMEN

OMAN

Karachi

New Delhi

GANGES R.

INDIA

BANGLADESH

Calcutta

BURMA

Hanoi

GULF OF ADEN

AFRICA

ARABIAN SEA

N

Bombay

Hyderabad

BAY OF BENGAL

Rangoon

Bangkok

THAILAND

LAOS

VIETNAM

SOUTH CHINA SEA

Manila

PHILIPPINES

Madras

CAMBODIA

Ho Chi Minh City

MEKONG

Celebes

SEYCHELLES

Cape Comorin

SRI LANKA
(CEYLON)

Colombo

MALDIVES

Malay Pen.

MALAYSIA

BRUNEI
(Br.)

Borneo

Kuala Lumpur

SINGAPORE

INDONESIA

INDIAN

Equator

SUNDA

Sumatra

Java   Surabaja

Timor

OCEAN

BRITISH INDIAN OCEAN TERRITORY

Djakarta

ISLANDS

Madagascar

MAURITIUS

AUSTRALIA

South Tropic Line
(Tropic of Capricorn)

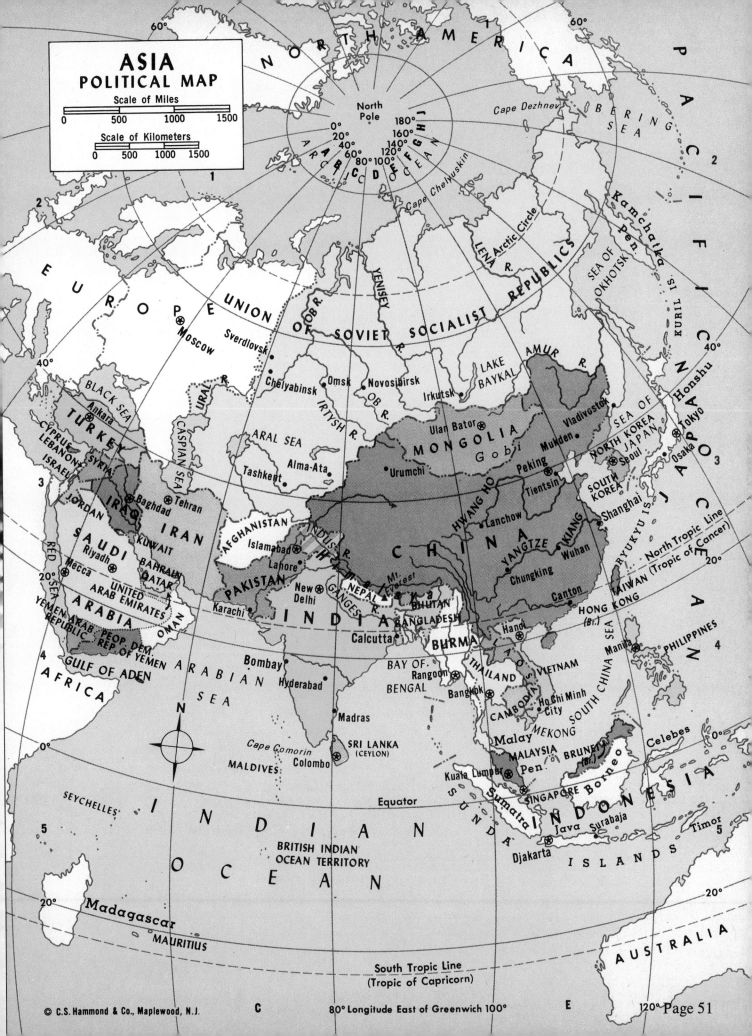

80° Longitude East of Greenwich 100°

ASIA

VEGETATION

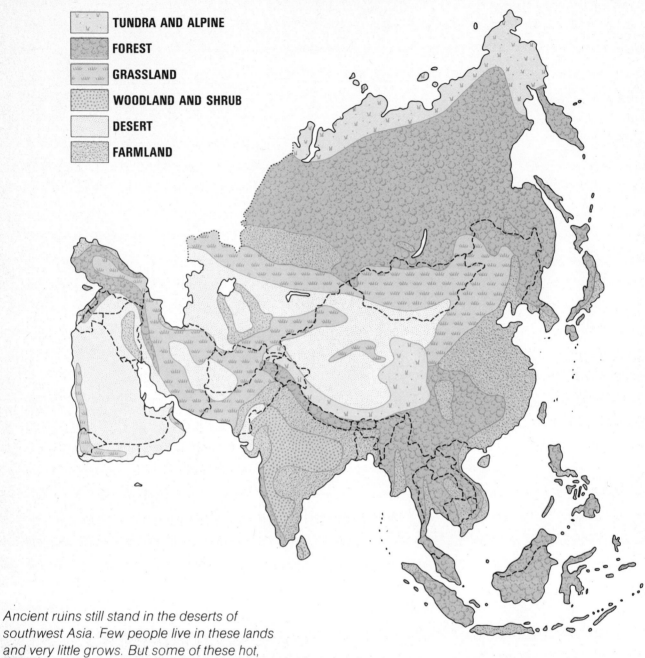

- ᴠ ᴠ **TUNDRA AND ALPINE**
- **FOREST**
- **GRASSLAND**
- **WOODLAND AND SHRUB**
- **DESERT**
- **FARMLAND**

Ancient ruins still stand in the deserts of southwest Asia. Few people live in these lands and very little grows. But some of these hot, dry areas have important oil fields.

Some areas of Asia have fertile soils. In these places, farming is very important. This farmer is growing rice—Asia's chief food crop. Most farms are small. Most work is done by hand.

POPULATION

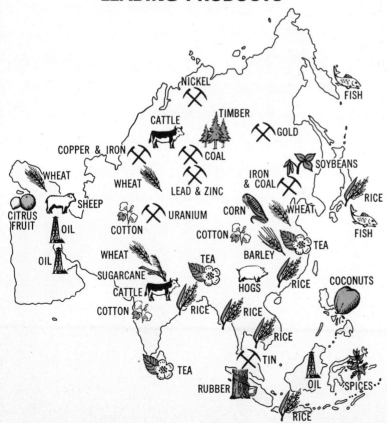

VERY CROWDED LANDS

CROWDED LANDS

LESS CROWDED LANDS

ALMOST EMPTY LANDS

LEADING PRODUCTS

NICKEL

FISH

CATTLE

TIMBER

GOLD

COPPER & IRON

COAL

SOYBEANS

IRON & COAL

WHEAT

LEAD & ZINC

RICE

WHEAT

URANIUM

CORN

WHEAT

CITRUS FRUIT

SHEEP

COTTON

COTTON

FISH

OIL

TEA

WHEAT

TEA

BARLEY

OIL

SUGARCANE

HOGS

RICE

CATTLE

COCONUTS

COTTON

RICE

RICE

RICE

TEA

TIN

RUBBER

OIL

SPICES

RICE

Tokyo, Japan's capital, is the world's second largest city. It has tall buildings and busy streets. It has helped Japan become an industrial giant.

Asia has many cities that are overcrowded. This street is in Bombay, India. What traffic problems can you see here?

Some Asian cities have large supermarkets. But in most places farmers bring their crops into town and sell them in open markets.

Page 53

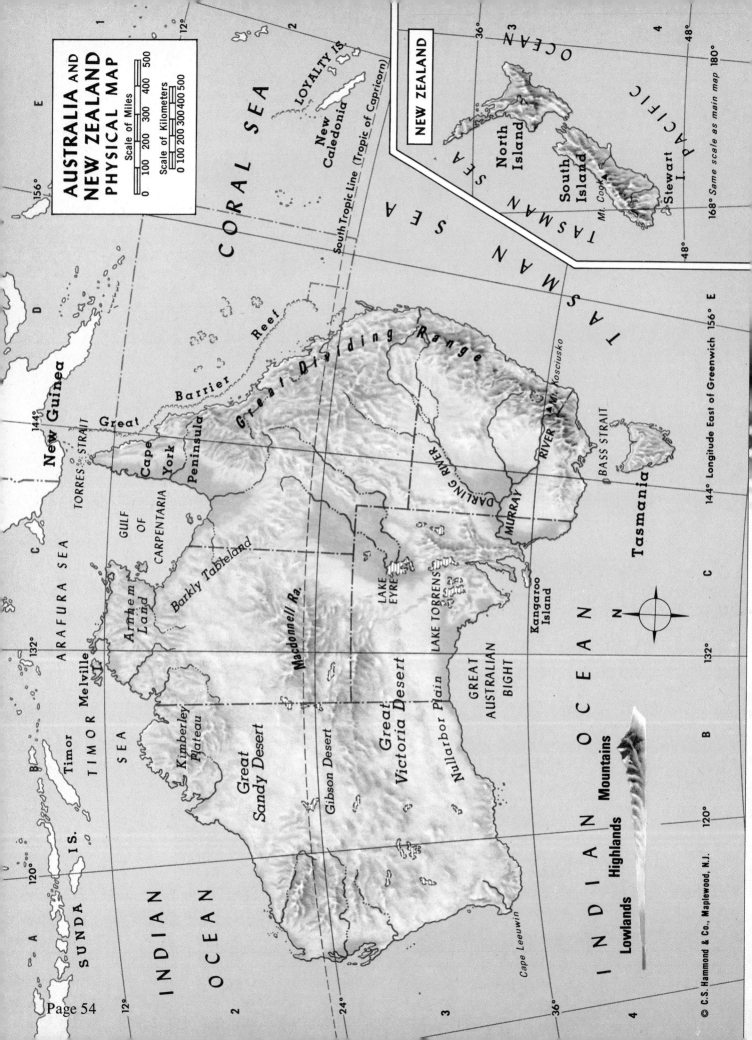

AUSTRALIA AND NEW ZEALAND PHYSICAL MAP

Scale of Miles
0 100 200 300 400 500

Scale of Kilometers
0 100 200 300 400 500

CORAL SEA

LOYALTY IS.

New Caledonia

South Tropic Line (Tropic of Capricorn)

NEW ZEALAND

OCEAN

North Island

South Island

Mt. Cook

Stewart I.

PACIFIC

TASMAN SEA

168° Same scale as main map 180°

New Guinea

Great Barrier Reef

Great Dividing Range

TORRES STRAIT

Cape York Peninsula

GULF OF CARPENTARIA

Arnhem Land

Barkly Tableland

Macdonnell Ra.

LAKE EYRE

LAKE TORRENS

DARLING RIVER

MURRAY RIVER

Mt. Kosciusko

BASS STRAIT

Tasmania

144° Longitude East of Greenwich 156° E

ARAFURA SEA

Timor

Melville

SUNDA IS.

TIMOR SEA

Kimberley Plateau

Great Sandy Desert

Gibson Desert

Great Victoria Desert

Nullarbor Plain

GREAT AUSTRALIAN BIGHT

Kangaroo Island

Cape Leeuwin

INDIAN OCEAN

N

Mountains

Highlands

Lowlands

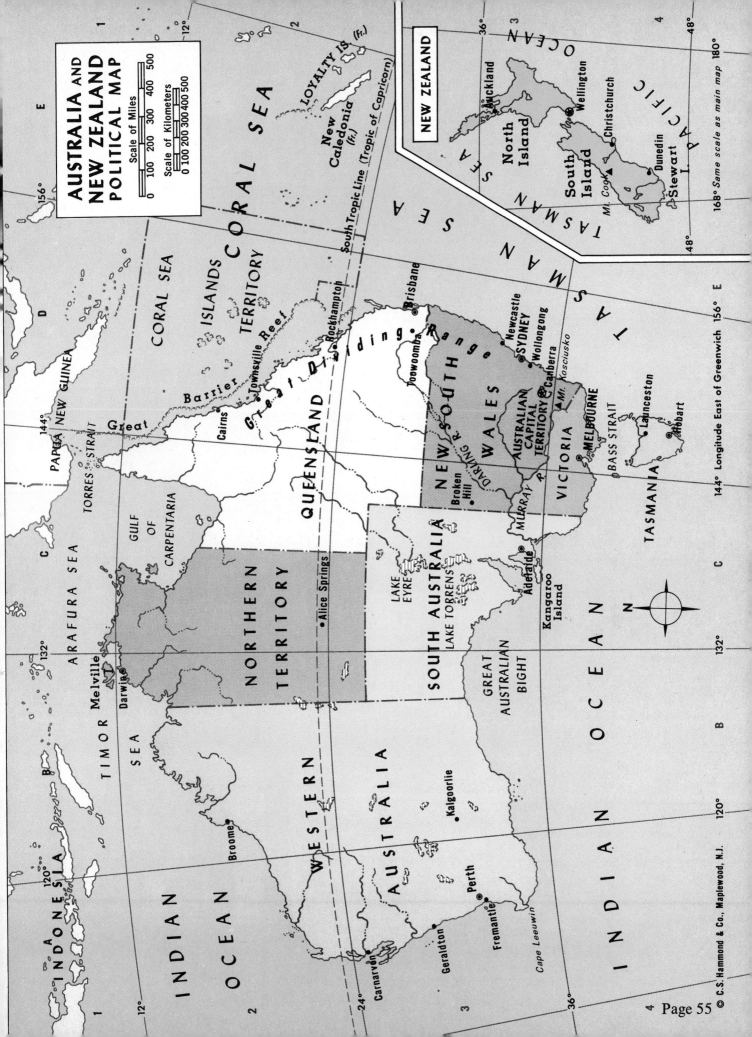

AUSTRALIA AND NEW ZEALAND POLITICAL MAP

Scale of Miles
0 100 200 300 400 500

Scale of Kilometers
0 100 200 300 400 500

NEW ZEALAND

PACIFIC OCEAN

Auckland

North Island

Wellington
Christchurch

TASMAN SEA

South Island
Mt. Cook
Dunedin
Stewart I.

168° *Same scale as main map.* 180°

48°
36°

INDONESIA

TIMOR SEA

ARAFURA SEA

PAPUA NEW GUINEA

TORRES STRAIT

GULF OF CARPENTARIA

Darwin
Melville I.

CORAL SEA

CORAL SEA ISLANDS TERRITORY

Great Barrier Reef

Cairns

Townsville

LOYALTY IS. (Fr.)

New Caledonia (Fr.)

South Tropic Line (Tropic of Capricorn)

Rockhampton
Brisbane

Doowoomba

Great Dividing Range

NORTHERN TERRITORY

Alice Springs

QUEENSLAND

WESTERN AUSTRALIA

Broome

SOUTH AUSTRALIA

LAKE EYRE

LAKE TORRENS

Broken Hill

NEW SOUTH WALES

Newcastle
SYDNEY
Wollongong
Canberra
AUSTRALIAN CAPITAL TERRITORY
Mt. Kosciusko

DARLING R.

MURRAY R.

VICTORIA

MELBOURNE

BASS STRAIT

Launceston

Hobart

TASMANIA

Adelaide

Kangaroo Island

GREAT AUSTRALIAN BIGHT

Kalgoorlie

Perth
Fremantle
Geraldton
Carnarvon
Cape Leeuwin

INDIAN OCEAN

N

© C.S. Hammond & Co., Maplewood, N.J.

Page 55

AUSTRALIA AND NEW ZEALAND

VEGETATION

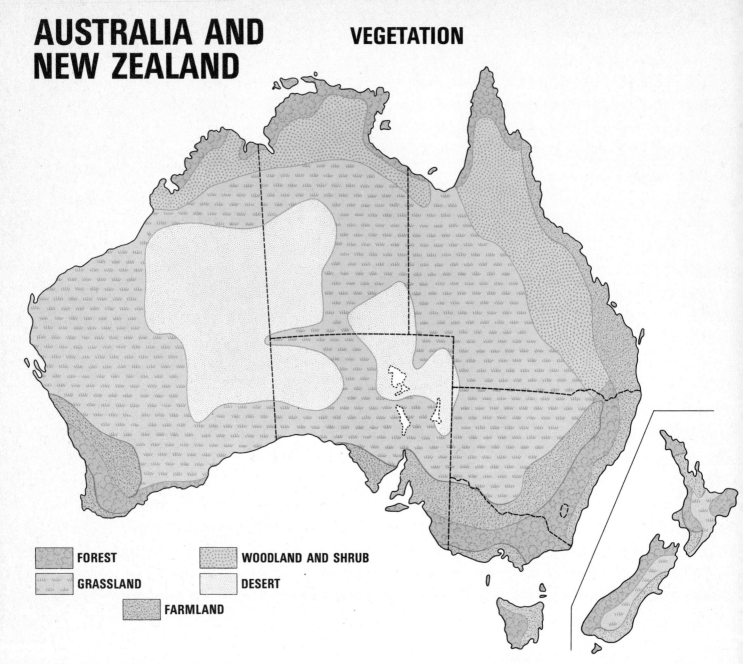

FOREST

GRASSLAND

WOODLAND AND SHRUB

DESERT

FARMLAND

Australia is a continent, an island, and a nation. The western half of Australia is a vast plateau. Much of the plateau is a desert. Yet many valuable minerals are found here.

New Zealand is a beautiful land. Its features include volcanoes, deep fiords, and snowcapped mountains.

POPULATION

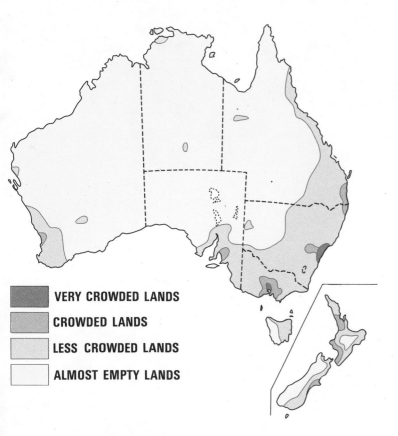

- ◼ VERY CROWDED LANDS
- ◼ CROWDED LANDS
- ◻ LESS CROWDED LANDS
- ◻ ALMOST EMPTY LANDS

LEADING PRODUCTS

Sydney is a port on Australia's southeast coast. Most Australians live in this region.

Wheat is Australia's main agricultural product. It is grown on about half of Australia's farmland. Sheep-raising is another important occupation.

Australia has many strange-looking animals. This is a koala and cub. Why do you think some animals are found only in Australia?

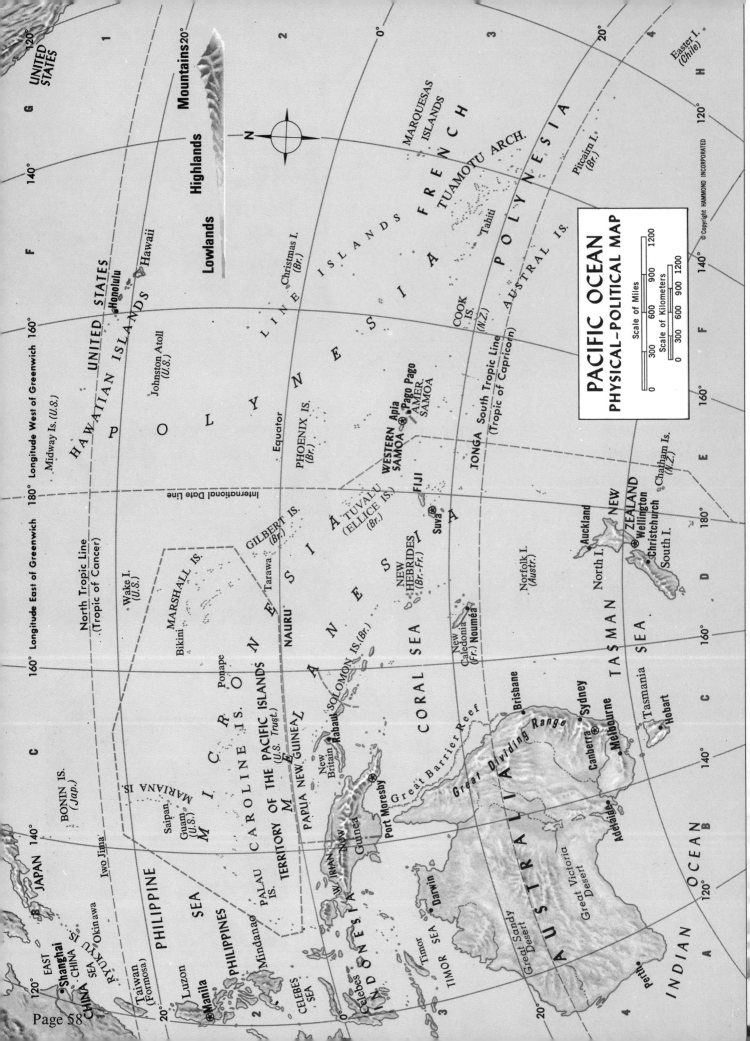

PACIFIC OCEAN
PHYSICAL–POLITICAL MAP

Scale of Miles

0   300   600   900   1200

Scale of Kilometers

0   300   600   900   1200

© Copyright HAMMOND INCORPORATED

Mountains

Highlands

Lowlands

UNITED STATES

Easter I. (Chile)

Pitcain I. (Br.)

MARQUESAS ISLANDS

TUAMOTU ARCH.

F R E N C H

P O L Y N E S I A

Tahiti

ISLANDS

AUSTRAL IS.

COOK IS. (N.Z.)

South Tropic Line (Tropic of Capricorn)

P O L Y N E S I A

Chatham Is. (N.Z.)

Christmas I. (Br.)

Line

Equator

Christmas I. (Br.)

PHOENIX IS. (Br.)

Apia
WESTERN SAMOA
Pago Pago
AMER. SAMOA

TONGA

Johnston Atoll (U.S.)

HAWAIIAN ISLANDS

UNITED STATES

Honolulu
Hawaii

Midway Is. (U.S.)

Longitude West of Greenwich

P O L Y N E S I A

International Date Line

North Tropic Line (Tropic of Cancer)

Longitude East of Greenwich

Wake I. (U.S.)

MARSHALL IS.

Bikini

GILBERT IS. (Br.)

Tarawa

TUVALU (ELLICE IS.) (Br.)

FIJI

Suva

NEW ZEALAND

Wellington

Auckland

North I.

South I.

Christchurch

NEW HEBRIDES (Br.-Fr.)

Norfolk I. (Austr.)

M E L A N E S I A

NAURU

SOLOMON IS. (Br.)

New Caledonia (Fr.) Nouméa

New Britain

Rabaul

New Ireland

PAPUA NEW GUINEA

Port Moresby

W. IRIAN

New Guinea

CORAL SEA

Great Barrier Reef

TASMAN SEA

TERRITORY OF THE PACIFIC ISLANDS (U.S. Trust.)

CAROLINE IS.

M I C R O N E S I A

Ponape

PALAU IS.

MARIANA IS.

Saipan
Guam (U.S.)

BONIN IS. (Jap.)

Iwo Jima

PHILIPPINE SEA

PHILIPPINES

Luzon

Manila

Mindanao

CELEBES SEA

I N D O N E S I A

Timor

TIMOR SEA

Darwin

Great Sandy Desert

Great Victoria Desert

A U S T R A L I A

Adelaide

Perth

Great Dividing Range

Brisbane

Sydney

Canberra

Melbourne

Tasmania

Hobart

INDIAN OCEAN

JAPAN

Shanghai
CHINA

Okinawa
RYUKYU IS.

Taiwan (Formosa)

EAST CHINA SEA

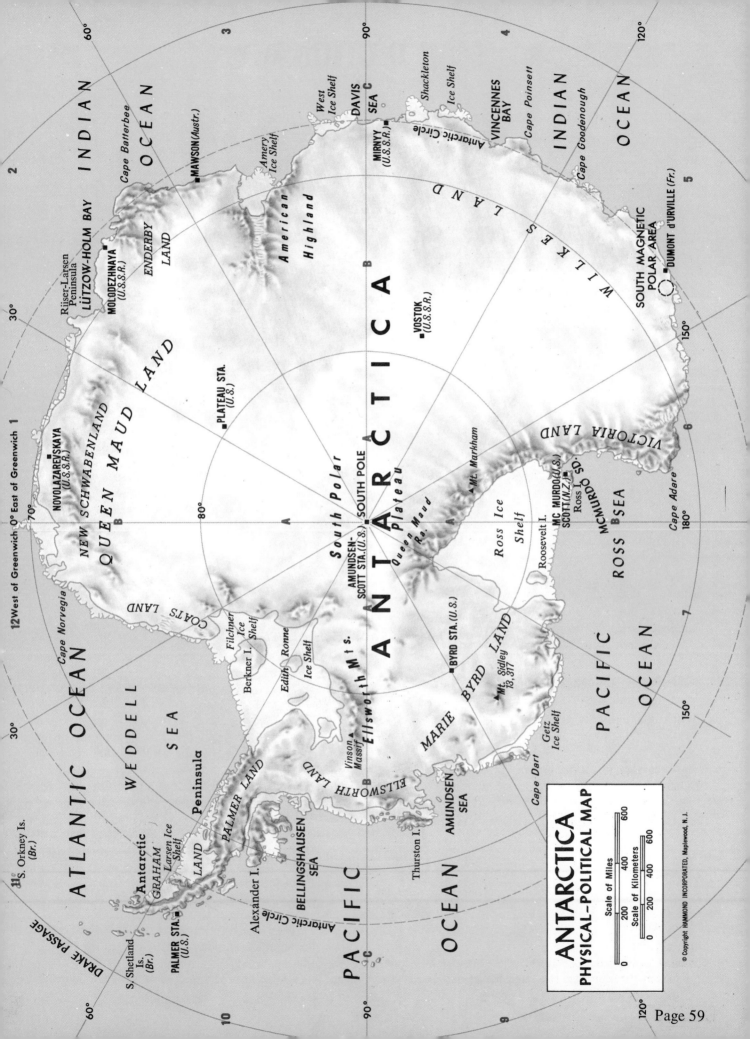

INDIAN OCEAN

ATLANTIC OCEAN

PACIFIC OCEAN

PACIFIC OCEAN

INDIAN OCEAN

DRAKE PASSAGE

S. Orkney Is. (Br.)

S. Shetland Is. (Br.)

Cape Norvegia

Cape Batterbee

60°
30°
0°
30°
60°
90°
120°
150°
180°
150°
120°
90°

2
3
4
5
6
7
9
10
11

12 West of Greenwich 0° East of Greenwich 1

West Ice Shelf

DAVIS SEA

MIRNYY (U.S.S.R.)

Shackleton Ice Shelf

Antarctic Circle

VINCENNES BAY

Cape Poinsett

Cape Goodenough

SOUTH MAGNETIC POLAR AREA

DUMONT d'URVILLE (Fr.)

Riiser-Larsen Peninsula

LÜTZOW-HOLM BAY

MOLODEZHNAYA (U.S.S.R.)

MAWSON (Austr.)

Amery Ice Shelf

ENDERBY LAND

American Highland

NOVOLAZAREVSKAYA (U.S.S.R.)

NEW SCHWABENLAND

QUEEN MAUD LAND

VOSTOK (U.S.S.R.)

PLATEAU STA. (U.S.)

WILKES LAND

WEDDELL SEA

COATS LAND

Filchner Ice Shelf

Berkner I.

Edith Ronne Ice Shelf

South Polar Plateau

SOUTH POLE

AMUNDSEN-SCOTT STA. (U.S.)

ANTARCTICA

Queen Maud Ra.

▲ Mt. Markham

VICTORIA LAND

Cape Adare

Antarctic

GRAHAM

Larsen Ice Shelf

Peninsula

PALMER STA. (U.S.)

PALMER LAND

Alexander I.

Antarctic Circle

BELLINGSHAUSEN SEA

Thurston I.

AMUNDSEN SEA

Cape Dart

Getz Ice Shelf

Vinson Massif ▲

Ellsworth Mts.

ELLSWORTH LAND

BYRD STA. (U.S.)

▲ Mt. Sidley 13,317

MARIE BYRD LAND

Ross Ice Shelf

Roosevelt I.

ROSS SEA

MC MURDO (U.S.)
SCOTT (N.Z.)
Ross I.
MCMURDO SD.

ANTARCTICA
PHYSICAL–POLITICAL MAP

Scale of Miles
0   200   400   600

Scale of Kilometers
0   200   400   600

© Copyright HAMMOND INCORPORATED, Maplewood, N.J.

Page 59

MAP DICTIONARY

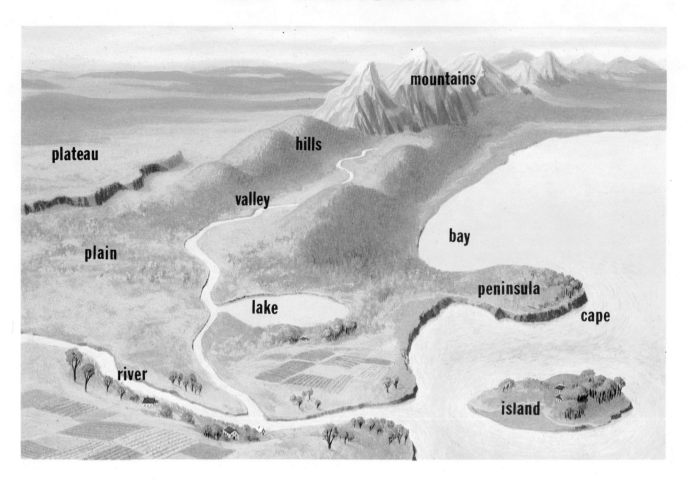

altitude — the height or elevation above sea level.

Antarctic Circle — an imaginary line of latitude 66°30′ (66 degrees, 30 minutes) south of the equator.

archipelago — a group or chain of islands.

Arctic Circle — an imaginary line of latitude 66°30′ north of the equator.

bay — an arm of an ocean, sea, or lake extending into land.

canal — a narrow, man-made waterway used for ships or irrigation.

canyon — a deep, narrow valley with steep, sloping sides.

cape (or point) — a point of land extending into a body of water.

channel — a narrow passage of water between two land-masses that connects two large bodies of water. Also, the deepest part of a river or harbor.

degree — one of the 360 units of measurement which make up a circle, represented by the symbol °. Degrees are subdivided into 60 minutes, represented by the symbol ′.

delta — a triangular or fan-shaped area of soil that has been carried downstream and dropped at a river's mouth.

depression — a land area that is lower than the surrounding ground. A depression is often below sea level.

desert — a land area so dry that little or no plant life will grow. Very few people live in a desert.

Eastern Hemisphere — the half of the earth that includes Africa, Asia, Australia, Europe, and their waters.

Equator — an imaginary line of latitude (0°) halfway between the North and South poles.

glacier — a large body of ice that moves slowly down a mountainside or along a valley toward sea level.

gulf — a large arm of an ocean or sea partly surrounded by land.

highland — a high or hilly area of land.

hill — a slightly higher point of land rising above the surrounding land.

ice shelf — a thick, floating area of ice lying next to a land area.

International Date Line — an imaginary line of longitude generally 180° east or west of the prime meridian. The date becomes one day earlier to the east of the line.

island — an area of land, smaller than a continent, completely surrounded by water.

isthmus — a narrow strip of land located between two water bodies, connecting two larger land areas.

lagoon — a shallow area of water separated from the ocean by a sandbank or by a strip of low land.

lake — a body of fresh or salt water entirely surrounded by land.

latitude — distance measured in degrees north or south of the equator.

longitude — distance measured in degrees east or west of the prime meridian.

meridian — an imaginary line of longitude running between the North Pole and South Pole.

mountain — an unusually high elevation rising steeply above its surroundings.

North Pole — the point farthest north on the earth's surface. It is 90° north of the equator.

North Tropic Line (or Tropic of Cancer) — an imaginary line of latitude 23°30′ north of the equator.

oasis — a spot in a desert made fertile by the presence of water.

ocean — one of the large areas of the earth into which the water surface is divided.

parallel — latitude line running east and west around the earth parallel to the equator.

peak — the highest point of a mountain.

peninsula — a piece of land extending into the sea almost surrounded by water.

plain — a flat or level area of land.

plateau (or tableland) — an elevated area of mostly level land, sometimes containing deep canyons.

population — the number of people. or inhabitants, living in a country, a city or town, or a particular area.

range (or mountain range) — a group or chain of high elevations.

reef — a chain of coral rocks or ridge of sand lying at or near the surface of a body of water.

reservoir — a man-made lake where water is kept for future use.

river — a large stream of water which flows on the earth's surface.

sea — a large body of salt water smaller than an ocean.

sea level — the surface level of the oceans. It is the same all over the world.

South Pole — the point farthest south on the earth's surface. It is 90° south of the equator.

South Tropic Line (or Tropic of Capricorn) — an imaginary line of latitude 23°30′ south of the equator.

strait — a narrow body of water connecting two larger bodies of water.

swamp — a low area of wet, spongy ground.

valley — a long, narrow land area lying between two areas of higher elevation. A valley usually contains a river or stream.

vegetation — all the different kinds of plant life that grow on the earth's surface.

volcano — a cone-shaped mountain that has an opening in the earth's crust from which lava can flow.

waterfall — a sudden drop of a stream from a high level to a much lower level.

Western Hemisphere — the half of the earth that includes North America, South America, and their waters.

THE WORLD'S CONTINENTS BY SIZE

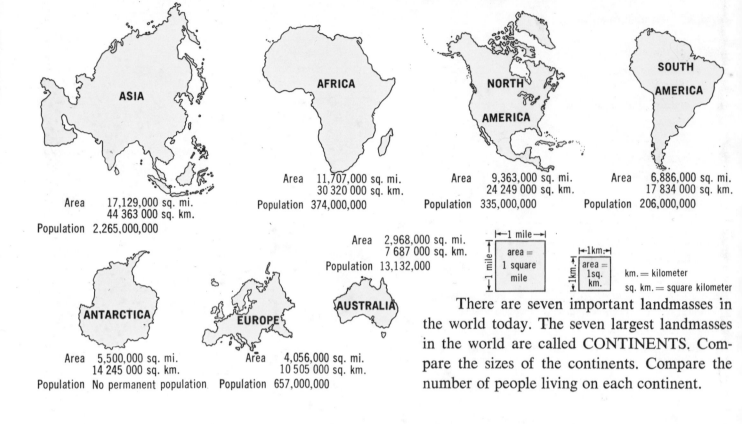

ASIA
Area   17,129,000 sq. mi.
44 363 000 sq. km.
Population   2,265,000,000

AFRICA
Area   11,707,000 sq. mi.
30 320 000 sq. km.
Population   374,000,000

NORTH AMERICA
Area   9,363,000 sq. mi.
24 249 000 sq. km.
Population   335,000,000

SOUTH AMERICA
Area   6,886,000 sq. mi.
17 834 000 sq. km.
Population   206,000,000

Area   2,968,000 sq. mi.
7 687 000 sq. km.
Population   13,132,000

ANTARCTICA
Area   5,500,000 sq. mi.
14 245 000 sq. km.
Population   No permanent population

EUROPE
Area   4,056,000 sq. mi.
10 505 000 sq. km.
Population   657,000,000

AUSTRALIA

area = 1 square mile   1 mile

area = 1 sq. km.   1 km.

km. = kilometer
sq. km. = square kilometer

There are seven important landmasses in the world today. The seven largest landmasses in the world are called CONTINENTS. Compare the sizes of the continents. Compare the number of people living on each continent.

WORLD TIME ZONES

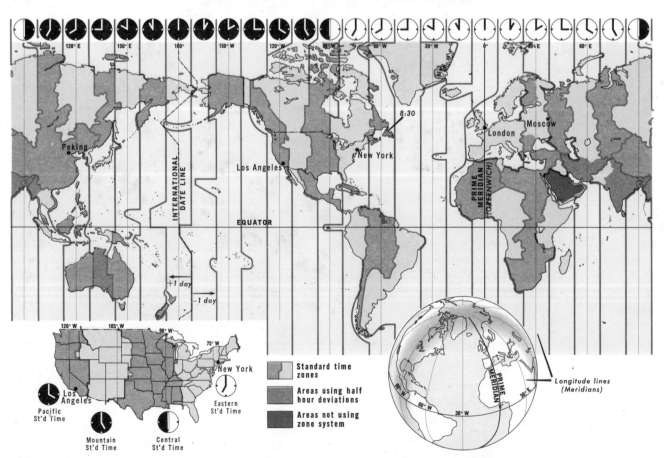

Standard time zones

Areas using half hour deviations

Areas not using zone system

Longitude lines (Meridians)